Dedication

Martha, my wife of over 40 years, a partner on two of these trips as well as many subsequent adventures all over the world.

And Wally Peterson who was on all three trips and joined me on ski trips in Europe and the Western U.S.

*To Larry
Enjoy
Rollie*

Acknowledgments

Wally Peterson's daughters who after his death in July 2, 1986, sent me his logs of the trips we had taken.

In 2014 as I read through them again I thought it was an interesting story.

Martha for helping with spelling, grammar, censoring, adding ideas, and providing her logs from the trips.

Eric Sevareid for his book "Canoeing with the Cree" and the inspiration it provided for the Hudson Bay Trip.

Sigurd Olson for his book *The Lonely Land* and meeting with us at his home in Ely, Minnesota before and after the Churchill River trip. He offered great practical advice and wrote beautiful descriptions of the land and river.

Bob O'Hara for planning the canoe rental, flights, and food for the Hudson Bay Trip.

The Hudson Bay Co for the one way canoe rental.

Cliff Wold in Ely, Minnesota for renting us an 18 foot canoe and letting us take it way up to Northern Saskatchewan.

Henry (Hank) Rempel, the Factor at Norway House Hudson Bay Post, for great hospitality, meals, a tour of Norway House, and the call for beer.

The employees of Gods River Lodge for a cabin one night and some great dinners.

Ross and Frazier, the Factors of the Hudson Bay Post in Shamattawa, for a warm house and a dry floor to sleep on when it rained.

Kent Stoephen for joining us on the Yukon River trip so we could travel with two canoes.

Phil Peterson Sr., a skiing friend who has written and published outdoor and adventure books, for giving me advice on how to turn my story into a book.

Cathy Wimmer for putting the book together.

Table of Contents

Prologue 1

PART 1: 1967

Chapter 1: I Join, and the Crew is Formed 3

Chapter 2: Getting There 5

Chapter 3: Norway House 7

Chapter 4: On Our Way 9

Chapter 5: Gods Lake 17

Chapter 6: Gods River 21

PART II: 1969

Chapter 7: What's Next 35

Chapter 8: On to the Churchill 39

Chapter 9: On the River 41

Chapter 10: The Mean Little Devil 57

Chapter 11: Out of the Woods 61

Chapter 12: What Next? 63

Part III: 1970

Chapter 13: The Inside Passage 65

Chapter 14: Getting to Whitehorse 67

Chapter 15: On the Water Again 69

Chapter 16: Dawson City 79

Chapter 17: Chilkoot Pass 85

Glossary

About the Author 94

Prologue

Paddling wild rivers of the north as a young person filled my mind with lifelong memories. The Gods River in northern Manitoba, the Churchill River in northern Saskatchewan and the Yukon River, in Yukon Territory, are three such rivers located in some of the most remote areas of Canada. Hiking over Chilkoot Pass from the Yukon Territory into Alaska gave me perspective on how challenging land transportation was and how difficult it was to get to the Klondike gold.

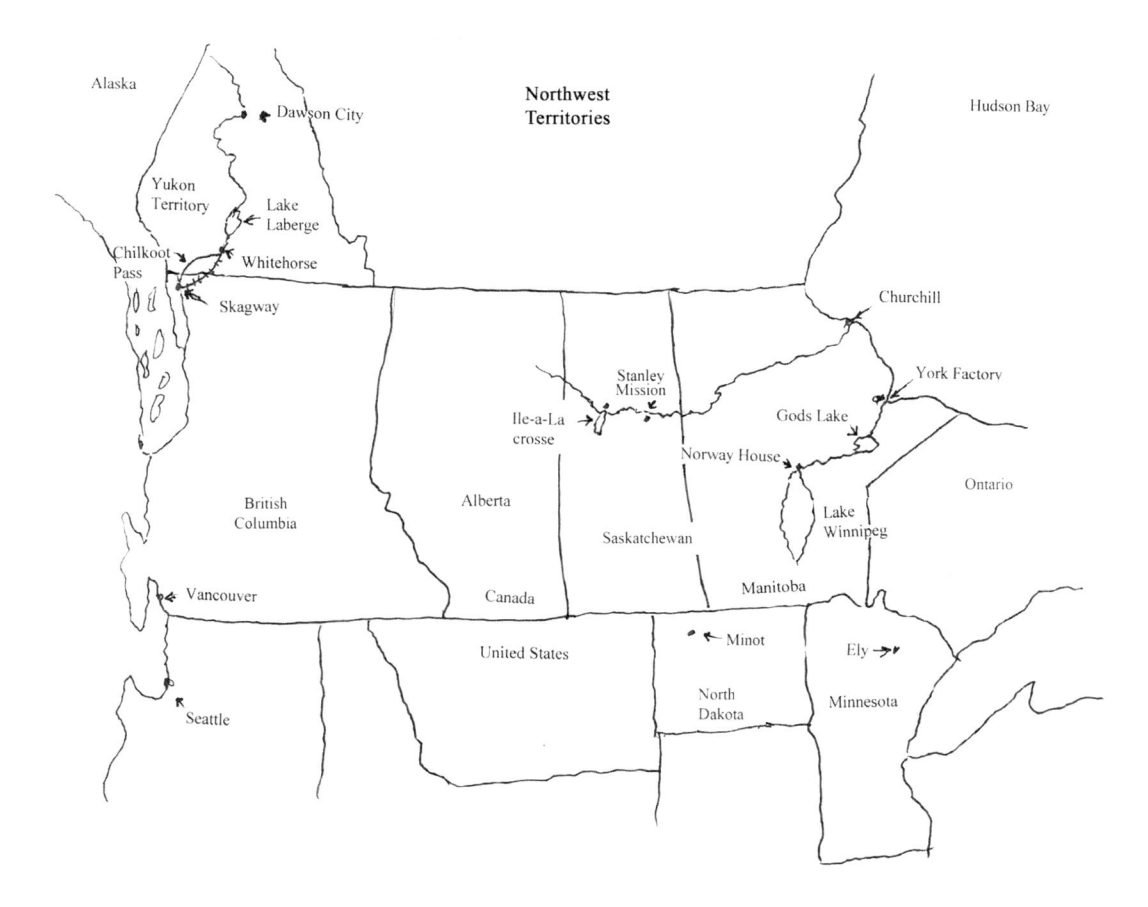

Our first trip was inspired by Eric Sevareid and Walter Post who had just graduated from high school in the 1930's and were looking for adventure. They decided to make a canoe trip from Minneapolis, Minnesota to Hudson Bay via the Minnesota River, the Red River, Lake Winnipeg, the Gods River and the Hayes River. Sevareid documented that trip in his book *Canoeing with the Cree*. The Cree are the Indians living in the area of Manitoba traveled by Sevareid and Post on this adventure. The book was published in 1935, years before Eric became famous as a newsman covering World War II. He won two George Foster Peabody awards for excellence in television newscasting while at CBS. During the war he parachuted out of a disabled airplane over Burma. Einar Anderson who also was on our trip was a pilot in Burma in World War II. Could Einar have been Eric's pilot in Burma?

Canoeing with the Cree has remained popular for more than three quarters of a century and has been reprinted nine times. The Minnesota Historical Society Press claimed to sell 1000 to 2000 copies a year. It has been the inspiration for many other adventures.

In the years since Eric and Walt made their trip, there have been others who have paddled similar routes. However, trips with modern gear and communication equipment are remarkably different experiences. For example, use of lightweight unsinkable covered canoes reduce the risks experienced in rapids and portages. Recently I read of two canoers doing the trip who were glad the sun came out so they could charge their cameras and satellite phone with their solar charger, a very different experience of solitude. There is a record of a trip like Sevareids, by Hudson Bay Expeditions, in which Dennis Smith led a group on the trip in a 26 ft. canoe. I guess there were enough members in the group to portage the large canoe.

The best section of the trip which Eric and Walt took is from Norway House on the north end of Lake Winnipeg to Hudson Bay via the Gods River. The section from Minneapolis to Lake Winnipeg ran mostly through developed farmland and passed many small towns. The members of the trip I took all had jobs and could not take off the whole summer. We decided to do the part of the trip from Norway House to York Factory on Hudson Bay. This section is mostly wilderness land and is filled with rapids and challenges.

Lake Winnipeg looked exciting to cross but we knew we could get wind bound for many days and get behind schedule. Eric and Walter tried to canoe Lake Winnipeg and had the wind problem. They got about halfway up the lake when the wind stopped them. As a result they took a freighter up to Norway House at the north end of the lake. That would be our starting point for our trip to York Factory on Hudson Bay. Bob O'Hara made arrangements for us to fly to Norway House from Riverton, Manitoba, a small town near Winnipeg with a seaplane base.

In 1969 Wally Peterson and I were eager for another wilderness canoe trip in the North. Martha Nelson, who I had met in Madison, Wisconsin, and I were fans of Sigurd Olson and we looked into the trip he describes in his book, *The Lonely Land* on the Churchill River in Saskatchewan, Canada. Without a partner for Wally we planned to use an 18 ft. canoe for the three of us and use Olson's book as our guide.

The next year, 1970, Wally, Martha and I made a plan to canoe the Yukon River in the Yukon Territory, Canada. The Gold Rush to Dawson in 1898 had intrigued us. After reading the wild accounts of that time, we decided to canoe the section of the Yukon River the men and women of the gold rush had traveled. A canoeing acquaintance of Wally's, Kent Stoephen, agreed to join us so we would travel with two canoes this time.

Once back in Whitehorse, after canoeing the Yukon, Wally, Martha, and I flew into Lake Lindeman and hiked over Chilkoot Pass from the Canadian side to Alaska to experience another chapter in the history of the gold rush.

Chapter One: I Join, and the Crew is Formed

Here we were at the "Powerhouse". That's what the locals call the municipal liquor store and bar in Lindstrom, Minnesota. We were there to have a couple beers after the wedding of a friend.

My good friend Wally Peterson was there. Wally and I had been on many ski trips in Europe and in the western U.S. He was one of the founders of Trollhaugen Ski Area in Dresser, Wisconsin. Wally was older and had canoed many rivers and lakes in Canada, Minnesota and Wisconsin.

While we were talking, he said, "Rollie you might be interested in the trip my son-in-law and some friends are planning. It's a canoe trip from Norway House at the north end of Lake Winnipeg to York factory on Hudson Bay. If you get a copy of the book *Canoeing with the Cree* by Eric Sevareid you can read about it. They plan to start from Norway House instead of Minneapolis where Sevareid and Post started.

I thought that sounded interesting. I am a water person having lived most of my life on a lake and I have competed in water ski competitions and performed in water ski shows. I've done a lot of swimming but not much canoeing other than at Boy Scout Camp and trips with rental canoes down the St. Croix River on a sunny afternoon. Wally thought I could handle the trip and would talk to his son-in-law, Curt Momson, whom I knew from when we both worked on the ski patrol at Trollhaugen Ski Area.

Because I was a musical instrument salesman and the summer is a slow time, I could take a month off to be part of the trip. In a couple of days I got the word that I could join the trip. It looked like a great group.

Bob O'Hara was in charge of making arrangements for the trip. He had done guiding in the Boundary Waters Canoe Area in Northern Minnesota and the Quetico Wilderness in Ontario,

Left to Right: Terry, Rollie, Wally, Curt, Bob, Einar, and Pete

Canada. He made arrangements for three rental canoes with the Hudson Bay Company and we would pick them up at Norway House at the north end of Lake Winnipeg and leave them at York Factory on Hudson Bay. He also arranged for the flight to Norway House from Riverton, Manitoba.

Bob was a classroom teacher, a cross-country ski coach, a graduate of St. John's University, and a recipient of two National Science Foundation grants for his graduate study in biology.

The other members of the group were:

Einar Anderson, a veteran of many years of wilderness canoeing. In World War ll he was a pilot in the China- Burma- India theater. A graduate of University of Minnesota and the county auditor in Brainerd, Minnesota, he has a deep interest in the early fur trade and Indian and Eskimo cultures;

Pete Humphrey, a banker at First Federal Bank in Brainerd and involved in Indian history and studies. Pete had traveled extensively by canoe in Canada and Northern Minnesota. Pete later left the bank after a 25 year successful career for his lifelong interest in Indian culture. He earned college credit from the Gods River Trip, and entered the American Indian studies program at the University Without Walls. After graduating he served as an adjunct faculty member at St. Cloud State University, earning a master's degree. He was made an honorary chief of the Leech Lake Ojibwe Band in 1972;

Terry McGaughey was in sales and had traveled many miles by canoe and bike. He is one of the founders of the Paul Bunyan bike trail in Minnesota. At the trailhead there is a plaque in his honor;

Curt Momson, a design engineer who had built many strip canoes in his day and was a member of the Minnesota Canoe Association. He was married to Wally's daughter;

Wally Peterson, the oldest of the crew at 59, had been a rural mail carrier before he and Lee Rogers started Trollhaugen Ski Area in 1950. In 1967 he and Lee sold Trollhaugen to Dr. Ray Rochford and Herman Ecklund. He loved to travel and he and I made numerous ski trips to Europe and even a side trip to Egypt in 1967; and myself, a graduate of the University of Minnesota in Geography and had served two years in the army and was working as a factory rep selling guitars and amplifiers. I also worked as a part time ski instructor on weekends at Trollhaugen.

Chapter Two: Getting There

On July 7, 1967, Wally and I left Center City and picked up Curt in Minneapolis. From there we took turns driving north. We stopped at an all night restaurant in Thief River Falls, Minnesota. The waitress had worked at the Flame Cafe in Minneapolis. She knew Leon Bollinger, leader of the house band there that used the guitar amplifiers that I sold. She said she liked living in northern Minnesota better than Minneapolis. People didn't talk to you or say hi in a big city.

We drove on toward Winnipeg. It was a straight highway through the flat land of the Red River Valley. Since we had a couple beers with supper we needed to stop along the road, but there were no shoulders. It was late so we pulled into a farm driveway, not a car for miles. We got out to relieve ourselves and here comes a lone car. Guess what, it pulled into the driveway where we were parked. We pulled out and they pulled into their farm home.

We drove all night across the border to Winnipeg and stopped tired and hungry at a restaurant along the road at about 6:00 a.m., only to find they didn't open until 7:00 a.m. So we had an extra hour of sleep in the car. After breakfast we headed toward Riverton. We stopped at Gimli, Manitoba. This is where Ernest Oberholtzer ended his 2,000 mile canoe voyage in 1912. The journal of that trip is published in *Bound for the Barrens* edited by Jean Sanford Replinger and published by Mallard Island Books. Ernest made the trip with Billy Magee an Ojibwe man older than him but experienced in traveling by canoe in Minnesota and Ontario in the early 1900's. They started at Le Pas (The Pas) and headed north as far as Hawkes Summit. From there east to Hudson Bay and down the coast past Churchill to York Factory. Then by river to Norway House and down Lake Winnipeg to Gimli. We would be canoeing to York Factory from the north end of Lake Winnipeg part of his trip but in the opposite direction.

We bought some bottles of rum and brandy for the trip. We poured it into plastic bottles we had with us from the pharmacy in St. Croix Falls, Wisconsin. This allowed us to avoid having to carry glass bottles and the plastic bottles we used again on another trip.

At Riverton we met the rest of the group. It was time to sort out our equipment. Everyone laid out all of their gear and we all had a chance to check it out. Comments like "why do you need this" or "we have four of them already" were heard. When we were done we had cut the gear in our packs by a fourth. Then to the local hotel for a couple beers and a steak dinner, maybe our last for a while. The plane arrived at 8:15 p.m.; we loaded up and flew over Lake Winnipeg to Norway House. Watching the lake from the plane we knew we were right to fly over it rather than trying to canoe it.

Arriving at 10:30 p.m., first thing we did was set up our tents in the field by the Norway House Fort and Hudson Bay Post. Some Indians came to see who we were. They were impressed when Pete and Einar sang and played drums to Indian songs that they knew. They invited us to a party and we said tomorrow night, because we were tired. Before bed we took a swim and found that the water is cold in the north country. We also found out how bad mosquitoes could be.

Map 1A

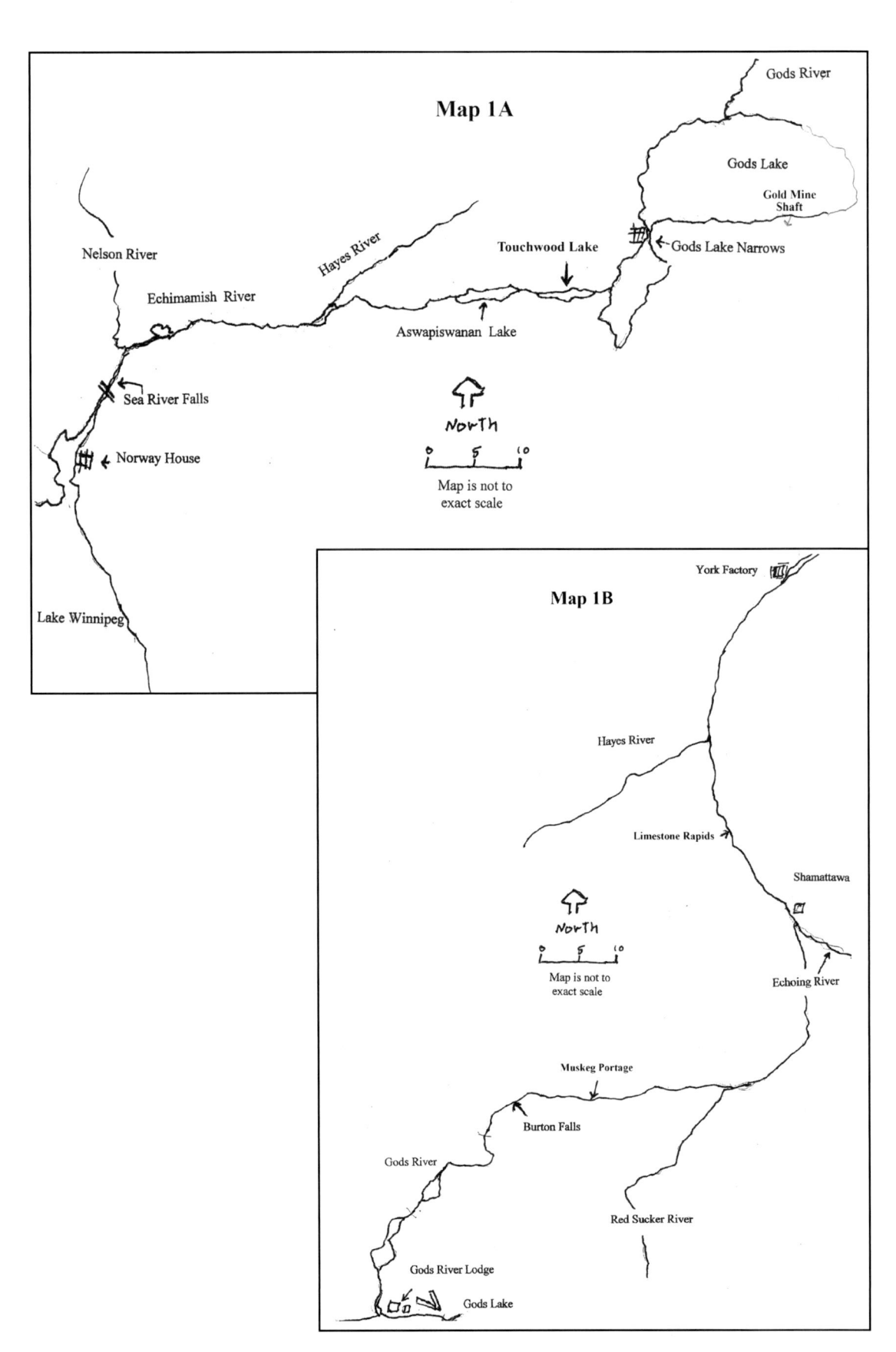

6

Chapter Three: Norway House

Got up in the morning about 8:00 a.m. Hank Rempel, the Factor at the Norway House Hudson Bay Post, had made breakfast for us. The managers of Hudson Bay Posts in Canada are called Factors. Almost every village in northern Canada has a Hudson Bay Post. They date back to the fur trade back of the 1800's, in many of the Canadian cities they have remained as department stores. The Hudson Bay Blanket is one of the famous items many people buy there.

Hank took us on a tour of Norway House: the school, the churches, the ranger station and the cemetery where we found small crosses on graves. We also found the small wooden form they used to make the cement crosses. At the cemetery we saw a grave that was marked Nancy Dease, wife of John Bell, Hudson Bay Company, died 15th September 1846, age 34. I bet life was tough in those days. On the grounds around the Post we found some old parts of broken clay pipes that the Voyageur's had used to smoke tobacco. Curt also found some square nails.

We went back to Hank's house by the Hudson Bay Company and had lunch, joined by Denny McKinney, from the conservation department. He recommended we avoid Oxford House and Bagley portage; the water there is shallow and we would have to do a lot of wading and pulling of the canoes. The Gods River he reported, was your best bet although it has a lot of rapids and waterfalls. This was the same advice that Eric and Walt received when they were at Norway House in the 1930's. So we would be traveling exactly the same route that they traveled on the Gods River to York Factory. Denny felt that the Gods River would be more exciting especially with the rapids we would be running. This sounded great as we all thought running rapids would be exciting and I was the only one who had not run rapids before. (See Maps 1a and 1b for our trips to Hudson Bay.)

The Canadian survey team guy with helicopter beer service

As we checked our maps and reviewed the route, someone said we needed a beer, but there are no beer stores in Norway house. Hank went to the phone and in a short time a helicopter landed in the backyard. Out jumped a member of a Canadian Survey team with two 12-packs of Canadian beer.

Are the Canadians friendly or what? Hank also told us about three canoes that were lost in the Gods River or the Hayes River. They washed up at York Factory. Now we worried a little. We talked and visited with Hank until about midnight. We agreed it was good that we had the rest day before the start of the trip.

The next morning, July 10th, we had breakfast with Hank, said our goodbyes and started for Hudson Bay. We stopped at a Conservation Department Headquarters for fishing licenses and check on the chance of forest fires along our route.

Chapter Four: On Our Way

We had a nice paddle along the Nelson River. We saw a batch of little ducklings and enjoyed a delicious lunch on a small rocky point. After lunch Curt took the bow of the canoe and I had my first chance to paddle in the back. How should I paddle in the back? Some of the group said to use the J stroke where you turn the paddle away from the canoe at the end of the stroke to keep it on a straight course. Others of the group said to use a rudder stroke where you turn the paddle toward the canoe to rudder it straight. To make everyone happy I did one style on the left and the other on the right. It was interesting that in a magazine article, published in 1980, by Sevareid about their 1930's trip Sevareid tells how the two of them paddled differently. Sevareid says he used an inward wrist-twist as the paddle emerged from each stroke, a rudder stroke. Post used a slight outward thrust of the blade, a J stroke.

We hit heavy wind about 2:30 p.m. so we went to the leeward side of an island and followed the north shore. Soon we could see the spray coming off Sea River Falls. As we came near we spotted an island in the middle of the falls. We landed on it and carried the canoes and gear over the island.

Pete and Einar lifting the canoe over the island at Sea River Falls

The river below the falls was wild with fast water and large waves. We put the canoes in at the bottom side of the island, loaded up, and carefully pushed off through the fast water. The big waves pushed us along and we all made it down to the quieter water. Present day canoeists are able to use the road from Thompson to the river below Sea River Falls and a ferry crossing. Some groups now start their trip to York Factory at the ferry instead of flying to Norway House.

We set up camp on an island. Wally caught a couple of walleyes for dinner. I landed a 5.5 pound northern pike (jackfish, as the Canadians called them) which we threw back. The Canadians call the northern pike jackfish. We looked at the following days route and I suggested we make sure we turn right on the stream that is the Echimamich River as there was another stream coming in that might confuse us. A couple of the guys commented that maybe I was a geography major in college, but they would know the right place to turn. We got to bed early to be ready for the next day.

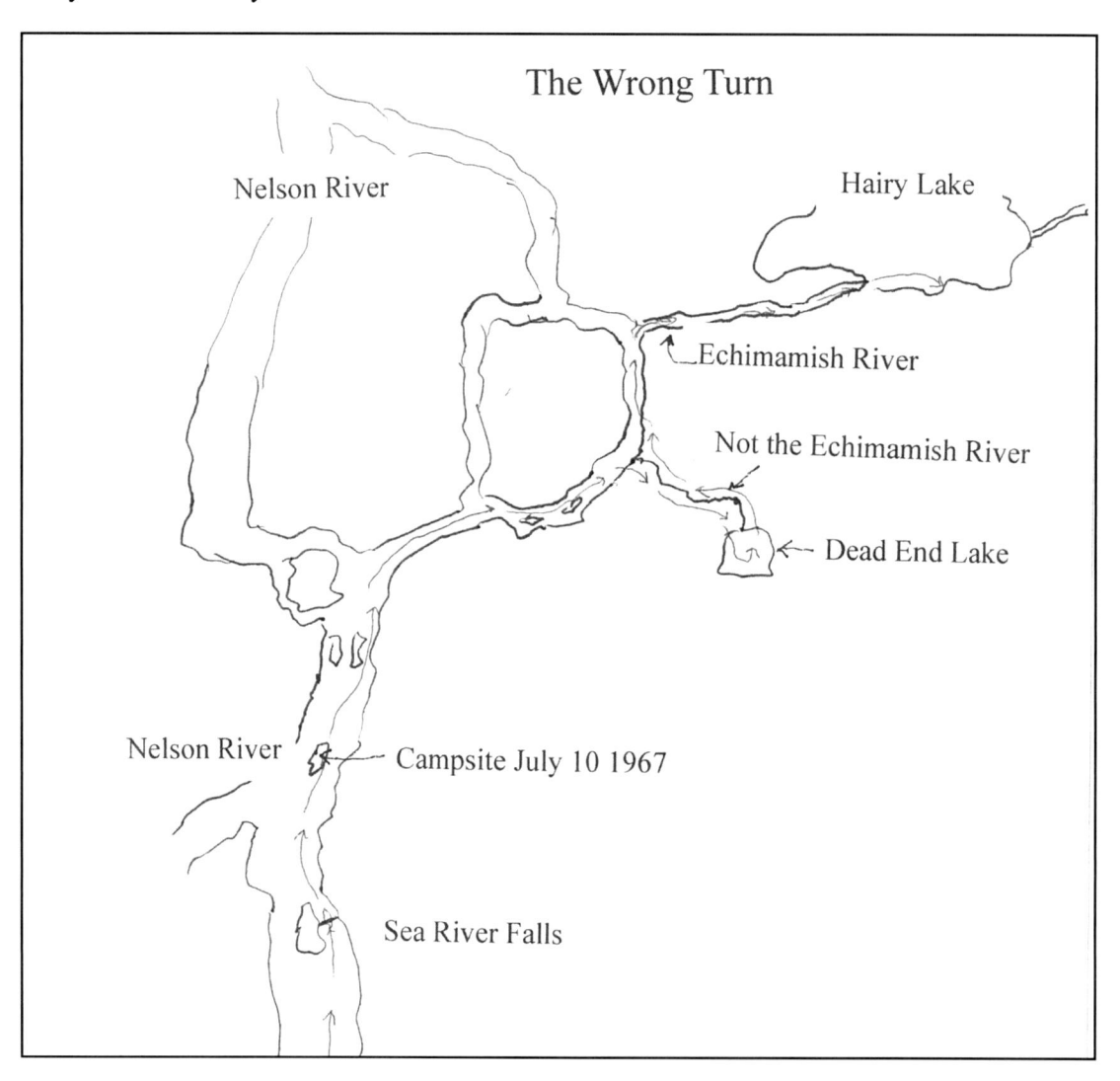

The Wrong Turn

- Nelson River
- Hairy Lake
- Echimamish River
- Not the Echimamish River
- Dead End Lake
- Nelson River
- Campsite July 10 1967
- Sea River Falls

We headed off in the morning in the drizzling rain and took the wrong turn. We went about two miles into a swamp, scouted from a ridge and saw no lake where it should be. I tried not to say "I told you so".

In 1930 Sevareid and Post also went up a wrong stream into a weedy lake with no exit. I wondered if they made the same wrong turn we did. The Echimamich River runs through Hairy Lake so we thought this swampy lake was Hairy Lake but we could find no exit. We canoed back to the Nelson River and in a few miles we found the Echimamich River. There was a sign

Pete and Einar think this is not the Echimamich

made by Indians that said Echimamich River. Below there was writing in Cree which we translated as "Go to God's Lake, go directly to God's Lake, do not pass go, do not collect $200.00."

The Echimamich River was not big and we had to carry over a portage and drag over a beaver dam. At the beaver dam there was no portage which made a tough job of dragging the canoes over it with all of the gear. We were paddling against a slow current and soon we got to the real Hairy Lake. It was full of weeds but easy to paddle through. Before long the wind was against us so we set up camp on the first rocky point we came to. We built a fire and had a chicken rice dinner. Curt told Terry to be careful of the slippery rocks on the shore. Terry went down to get a drink and slipped and fell in. Curt did not like having a wet tent mate. The group ended the night with hot drinks and Bob made cookies. Bob slipped when he carried the cookies and they flew, they were good but wet. We appreciated the hot drinks to warm us up and we all teased Bob about "tossing his cookies."

This swampy area was thick with mosquitoes. Wally and I devised a system to get into the tent without mosquitoes. You spray a cloud of repellent by the tent opening and then jump in quickly. It worked pretty well to keep the mosquitoes from coming into the tent with us.

The next morning we woke up to a sunny day, and ate oatmeal and peach compote for breakfast. We headed across Hairy Lake but stayed along the shore to avoid the wind. We stopped for lunch at a small clearing but the mosquitoes were so bad we climbed up on the ridge to eat. There was wind all day and that ended the problem of mosquitoes for a while. Most of us tucked our pants legs into our socks to keep the mosquitoes off our ankles. Pete, who is a big guy, had an opening at his waist between his shirt and pants that was full of bites from black flies and mosquitoes. He didn't complain but we were sure he suffered.

The next campsite had lots of grass and mosquitoes but it became our favorite site because the fishing was great.

Walleyes

    We caught one walleye after another and had a great fish meal. We caught about 30 walleyes and returned most of them to the river. Walking around the campsite, Terry fell into an old goose hunting blind. Luckily, he was not hurt. A minor injury on a trip like this could be a major problem. We also swam and washed clothes. The water in the river seemed warmer than in the lakes. The mosquitoes were bad again and put us to bed early.

    On July 13th we started early with no breakfast, after 45 minutes we stopped for breakfast at a rock ledge with fewer mosquitoes. We continued on to another rock ledge for a lunch site where we found the end of the river. Echimamich in Cree means "river that runs both ways". Now we would no longer be paddling against the current but joining the flow of the Hayes River, going the other way, with the current. It was a large flat area with a short portage over a slight rise, into a beautiful river valley. We stopped for a short break, then continued into the first lake on the route. We were paddling along in a small, calm lake when we heard a big roar coming down the lake. It was a tornado or a waterspout and it passed by our canoe. In a couple minutes the air was calm and not a ripple on the water. Was it a ghost or an Indian Spirit that lived in this country? We looked at each other and thought what if it had hit our canoes? Now there was not a cloud in the sky and no wind, where had it come from? We got to Robinson Lake but the campsite where we had planned to stay was unsuitable, so we went on to another point. It was better, had many dragonflies, and was more open. The dragonflies seemed to be eating the mosquitoes out of the air.

    On July 14th I woke to hear Wally and Pete talking about the fish Wally was catching. They were northern pike or jackfish as the Canadians call them. I got cleaned up and joined them fishing. I didn't have a metal leader so I lost a jackfish, it took my Rapala bait. Curt was also fishing in the same area and soon caught a jackfish and in his mouth was my Rapala that the fish had taken earlier.

Rollie pulling the canoe through the swamp

On our trip the Canadian topographic maps were excellent and we knew our exact location. Sevareid and Post apparently had aerial maps and they're not as accurate so they would count the strokes as they paddled to help them figure out where they were. At noon we arrived at a falls. We canoed as close to the falls as we could, then scouted the woods for a portage. We couldn't find one so we carried the packs through the woods past the falls. On the way back to the canoes I continued straight east and found a portage. So did Bob and Terry. We went back to the canoes and started to hike over the portage with the canoes. Wally slipped and strained his back, but fortunately was OK by the next day. After the portage we stopped and ate lunch.

The next portage into a small lake went fine. The Hayes River flowed out from this lake. If we were to go the Oxford House route we would go north from here, but we stayed on the route to the Gods River. We saw a moose on the next lake and had another portage with many mosquitoes. We found a campsite on the far end of the next lake. While supper was being made Wally and I caught some walleyes for breakfast. The mosquitoes were really bad and there was light rain at bedtime. The next morning we all enjoyed breakfast with the six walleyes Wally and I caught the night before.

Moving across the Canadian shield means going from one lake to the next. Many of the lakes have rapids or falls where the water flows into the next lake. We were able to find a portage around the next two rapids. Then came a problem; the next portage should have been a straight shot through the woods. All of us hunted but we found no portage. We saw it on the map but apparently it had grown over. A small stream flowed out of the lake and we dragged and pulled the canoes through the swamp and weeds to the next lake.

We got our feet wet and also had to wear nets over our heads because of the black flies. When we got to the lake both Curt and I felt this lake wasn't the right shape and we seemed to be too far north. I looked at the lake and it clearly was not what the lake looked like on the map. After checking the map again, Curt and I walked over the ridge on the south side of the lake and there was the lake shaped like the one on the map which we should be on. So we carried our gear and canoes up over the ridge into the other lake. It felt good to be on track again. One of the problems with these lakes is that they all look a bit alike and if you don't pay attention to your topographic map you can easily get into the wrong bay or stream. Then you could be lost and in trouble. (See Sketch #1.)

Once we got to the right lake it began to rain heavily. For a couple hours we were getting soaking wet. We made two more portages that were slippery and made camp on a long thin lake with some wind but not enough to stop the mosquitoes. Wally and I took a swim and Bob made some popcorn for everyone.

It was a cold, cloudy morning the next day. We started early and made it over two portages. We found an old trapper's shack with an old sled and some snowshoes hanging on the wall. After the next portage we came to a marshy area and heard some splashing. Around the corner was a large moose posing for us. Surprisingly, it didn't run off but calmly continued feeding on the lake weeds.

Next we came to Lake Aswapiswanan with a rocky point for lunch. What could have been a wind problem was a fantastic, calm, beautiful lake just for us. We took our time and paddled slowly, enjoying this pristine wilderness. It was calm as a mirror with the shore and the sky reflected perfectly on the surface of the lake.

Some people may wonder why would you go off into the mosquito infested wilds? Experiencing this fantastic lake and scenery says it all. And no mosquitoes in the middle of the lake.

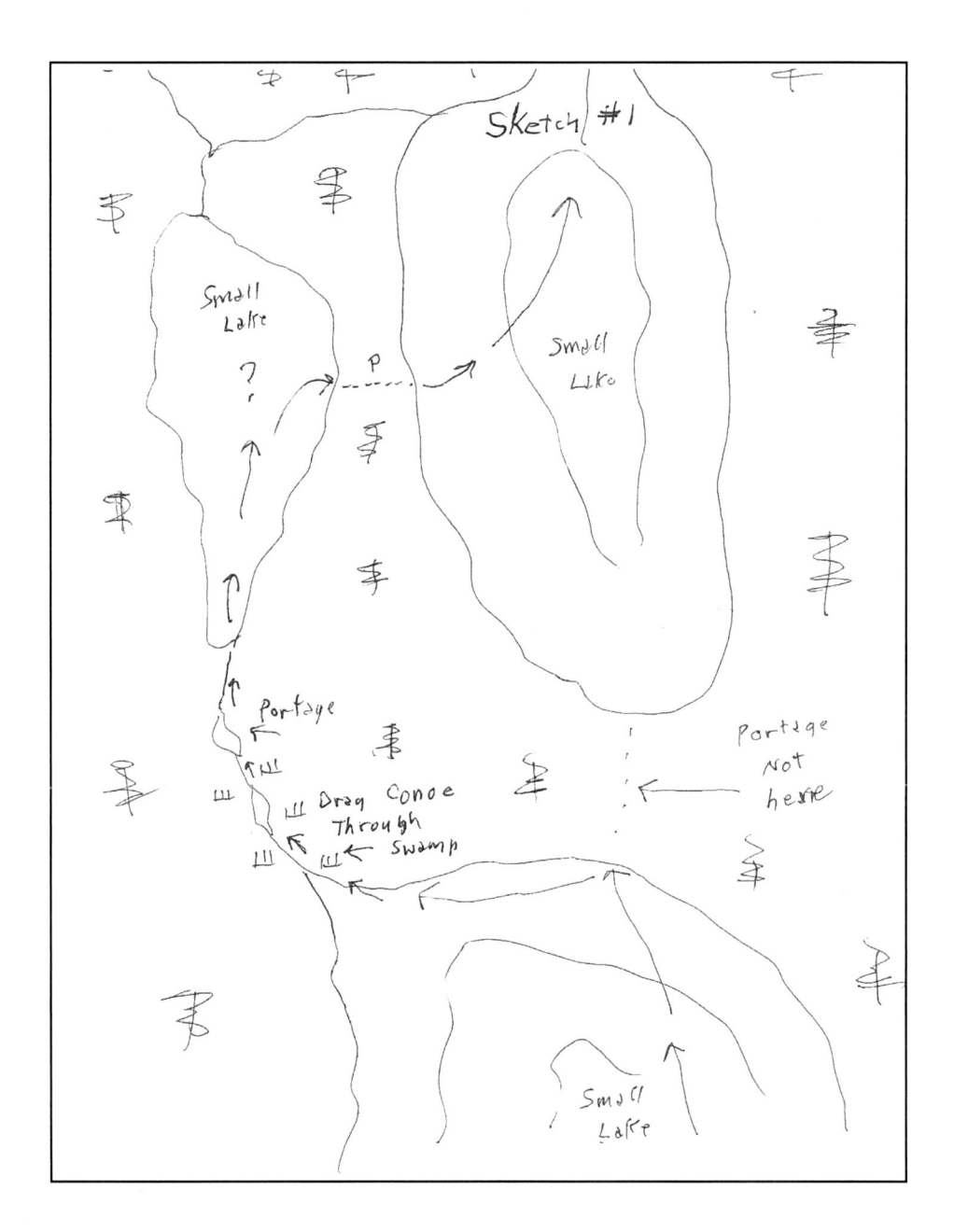

At the far end of the lake we looked for the next portage but could not find one. There was a clearing we had passed so we paddled back to it. There were mosquitoes again. The dragonflies flying past our faces seemed to be eating mosquitoes right out of the swarm that surrounded our heads.

    The next morning Curt and I got up early and paddled to where the portage was to be. We did a lot of walking in the brush full of mosquitoes but still no portage. This had not been my favorite campsite, no flat spots for our tent and lots of black flies. The rapids looked doable if we stayed to the right. When we got back to the guys they agreed to shoot the rapids on the right. The right side turned out fine with some large waves but no rocks. And after two more rapids we were now on our way down the Mink River to Touchwood Lake. We came down the

Lake Aswapiswanan

main part of the lake and stopped for lunch at a small island. The paddle across Touchwood Lake was calm, with no wind. Again, the sky and shore reflected beautifully on the lake.

It was the eighth day without seeing another person who was not one of us. Curt told the story of Chan the village craftsman who made small statues out of teak. One morning he came to his shop to find the window open and a couple of statues missing. On the ground outside there were footprints of a small child. With the help of the police they dug a hole outside the window and covered it with straw to try to catch the thief. The next night he heard a crash and in the morning, with the police, they looked in the hole. They were amazed at what they saw. A black bear with human looking feet, clutching several statues. The craftsman exclaimed "Ah, boy-foot bear with teaks of Chan". Peter almost fell out of the canoe he laughed so hard.

We found a nice campsite on the narrows into Vermillion Lake. We did some fishing but only caught jackfish (northerns) as we are now getting into an area where there are more people including fishermen who fly in from the U.S. We had been back in the wilds where few guides take their guests. We had supper of hash and beef and a couple of bumps before bed by 11:15 p.m.. Bumps are what we would call a small shot of brandy.

We got up about 9:30 a.m. to a beautiful day and we turned into the east channel into Gods Lake. We came to rapids and discovered we were in the wrong channel. We had a rough paddle to get back to Lake Vermilion. Then took the west channel which had two rapids, but we shot those. It was my first time in the back of the canoe running the rapids and I had watched Curt enough to get it just right. We could not find the portage around the last rapids, it was on the other side of the river so we shot the rapids and portaged over some rocks. The last rapids were fun. I was in the front and Terry in the back. It was a thrill to crash down the rapids with the view of Gods Lake ahead. The sun was shimmering off the lake, "Gods Lake." It met our expectations of what Gods Lake should look like.

Chapter Five: Gods Lake

The first name for the lake was Devils Lake because the Indians did not like how wild and devilish the waves could be. When the missionaries came they thought it too beautiful to be called devils so they changed the name to Gods Lake. God did add mosquitoes so it would not be overpopulated. In his book, Sevareid says, "I cannot imagine how a lake could be more thrillingly beautiful than Gods Lake. Such sights as this are reserved for those who will suffer to behold them." And all seven of us and our three canoes had made it so far.

Now we paddled a short distance to Gods River Narrows, an Indian village that I think was where Sevareid and Post landed. Gods River Lodge was not there at the time. Sevareid and Post were greeted here by barking dogs, children, and Crees wondering who they were. We had a similar greeting. The conservation office yard made a great place to set up our tents. The Hudson Bay post sold bacon and eggs for our breakfast. The conservation officer suggested we arrange to be towed across Gods Lake as it can get windy causing delays. We hired Thompson Trout to tow us and the three canoes. There would be no worry about wind on the big lake. There was a dance at the council room as is the normal event each night. They enjoyed Pete and Einar's Ojibwa music. We got to bed about 11:15 p.m. knowing we would have bacon and eggs for breakfast.

Our next stop would be Gods River Lodge, a resort for fisherman who fly in for the great fishing. As we were ready to go, Paul and Jeff, survey government workers checking on commercial fishing, said they were going to Gods River Lodge and if we were ready to leave Pete and I could ride with them. So Pete and I rode with them rather than cross the lake with

Crossing Gods Lake

Curt and Rollie doing rapids practice

Thompson Trout. We stopped at Burton's Lodge, met Pete Burton and got some information on the Gods River section of our trip. We rejoined the main party at the gold mine shaft. Then we went on and got to Gods River Lodge before the boat pulling the three canoes arrived.

Pete and I hit the lodge for apple pie and sandwiches as soon as we got there. Too bad for our friends in the motor boat towing the canoes across the lake.

I decided to do some fishing while we waited for the rest of the crew. I landed a whitefish that I was about to throw back when Paul said to get it weighed as it might be big enough to be an award. It was 4 lbs 6 ozs when registered, and that made me a Manitoba Master Angler. When Wally arrived I had to tell him that now I was a Master Angler. I frequently reminded him over the following years that I was a Master Angler, while he felt that a whitefish was not a real fish.

We arranged for steak dinners and stayed in an empty cabin with showers that night. We had flush toilets for the first time in weeks. That night we visited with the staff and had coffee in the lodge kitchen until 11:30 p.m. During the day we practiced the rapids by the lodge where the Gods River leaves Gods Lake. They are right by the lodge so we ran them over and over again for practice. That night about 2:30 a.m. there was a big thunderstorm and some wind so we ran out of the cabin, and took down our tents, folded them up and put them on the cabin porch. We had breakfast in the lodge at 8:00 a.m. then practiced the rapids by the lodge.

We had some upsets and some nice runs. Pete and Einar tipped and we got a boat to tow them back. Pete fell on a rock getting into the boat but was not hurt. Then we repacked our food and added food that had been in the packs we had flown into Gods River Lodge. In the 1930's Gods River Lodge was not there and there were no float planes to fly in supplies for Sevareid and Post. If we hadn't had the extra packs of food flown in, the food for seven guys for a month would have added significant weight to our canoe load.

We met Tom McKay, a 15 year old Indian boy, who had a guitar. He said we should go to the council room at about 9:00 p.m. for music. The seven of us, plus Isabelle from the lodge and Ray Peck, a bush pilot, drove in a pickup road down the old runway to the council room. Tom and I took turns playing the guitar and singing. Pete and Einar did some Ojibwe songs. Then the children sang "Jesus Loves Me". That was a big hit. Then lightning brought a halt to the fun and we did the long walk back to our tents. After I got back home I sent Tom a new set of guitar strings. He sent me a thank you note but said, "I hope you won't shoot me if I tell you that I quit school this fall because I didn't like the new teacher". He was sorry but he quit school and was going to work up north, in the mining area, so he could get married. He also said he had become a Christian that summer.

The cabins were all rented that night, so we had to get back into our tents. The thunder was so loud it seemed to move the ground around the tents. In the far north the storms and accompanying lightning and thunder seem stronger than in the Midwest.

After breakfast in the morning we waited for Tom Romanski who owns the God Rivers Lodge to return and give us advice on the trip ahead. Alex, an Indian guide, said we should have a guide with us. Tom Romanski returned and also said it's best to have a guide. We had a nice supper at the lodge then went to the village to sing and play songs for the children. After the fun of singing we returned to the lodge for coffee, then to the tents as the cabins were still rented. That night the lightning and thunder rocked the ground again and the tents leaked, but not too badly.

Eric and Walt had a hard time with Gods Lake. They had no topo maps; only a compass and some aerial maps to help them find the place where the Gods River runs out of the Gods Lake. They went by the tip of Elk Island and could tell it was the right island because it had been recently burned by fire. From there they headed across the 20 mile part of the lake heading straight north hoping to find the outlet of the Gods River. They landed on the shore a short distance to the east and felt from the current they were near the outlet. Gods River Lodge, a famous fishing resort, now stands at the location where the Gods River runs out of Gods Lake.

Chapter Six: Gods River

We started the next day with a hearty breakfast. The guide did not show up by 9:00 a.m., so we took off without him. The first rapids went well. On the next rapids we carried over on the left side of the falls, that way we didn't have to unload the canoes. It went OK as long as we had no slips or falls. The next rapids we portaged on the left then had clear sailing until Allan Rapids. The portages along here were not too bad as the fisherman from the lodge use them. Allen Rapids was tough on the right side with rocks and some big water. We ran them on the right and came close to crashing, but our skill, or luck, held and we just made it through. Sometimes rocks just under the surface are hard to see until you hit them.

Wally and I had luck fishing a little below Allen Rapids. As we paddled on we wondered about an old cabin on the shore; another untold story of the river. The paddling was nice all the way to the Pine Rapids where the Semmens River joins the Gods. Staying to the right through the first part of the Pine Rapids brought us to a rocky camp spot just above the gorge of the second part of Pine Rapids.

Near the campsite I found a place where there were a lot of rock chips. Pete, who had done Indian studies, thought a chipping rock, used to make arrowheads and tools, was located nearby. With Pete's help, we found the location of the chipping rock. That night, from our campsite, we could see smoke in the distance from a fire, but not close to where we were headed.

In the morning it was cold and windy when we got to the gorge. We scouted it and thought we could make it if we took it one canoe at a time while the others took pictures. We hated to portage if we could get by running the rapids. But if we lost a canoe, we would have seven guys

Wally cleaning Brook Trout

Wally and Bob watched as Pete tried to pull gear out of the canoe

and all our gear and food to put into two canoes. That would be a huge problem. Sevareid and Post would have an even bigger problem since it was just the two of them in one canoe. Later we passed Gods River Lodge's out-cabin for guests to stay temporarily while fishing the Gods River.

Now we should have great fishing because we were out of the area where the guides took the guests from Gods River Lodge. At lunch we stopped and Wally caught the first brook trout, so I owe him a six pack when we get back to civilization. He was proud to have out-fished a Master Angler. Now we were catching brook trout and walleyes on every cast. We had pinched the barbs on the hooks so we could release the fish more easily. With fishing this good we only kept fish to eat and released the rest.

I slipped on the rocks and got wet up to my waist, but no injury. I was just wet and cold. We continued on to some big rapids just above Burton Falls which we portaged on the left.

We stopped for lunch and checked the second section. It looked good on the left but as we got close Bob, in the front, motioned for us to go to the right. All of us turned. In going across the fast current, Pete and Einar tipped and floated down over small falls, hanging on to their canoe. The current brought them up against an island. Their canoe was wedged against the rocks. Water was pouring into the canoe as it was open to the full force of the current.

"I hope it doesn't break," Bob worried out loud. The rest of us turned back, up current, and paddled as hard as we could up and across to the left side of the river. We cut and made a rough portage along the left side to where we could put our canoes in the river below the island. Once in the river below the island, we paddled up to the backside of the island to where Pete and Einar were waiting. After landing we emptied the gear from their canoe. It still wouldn't come loose and was held fast due to the pressure of the current. After cutting a couple aspen poles to

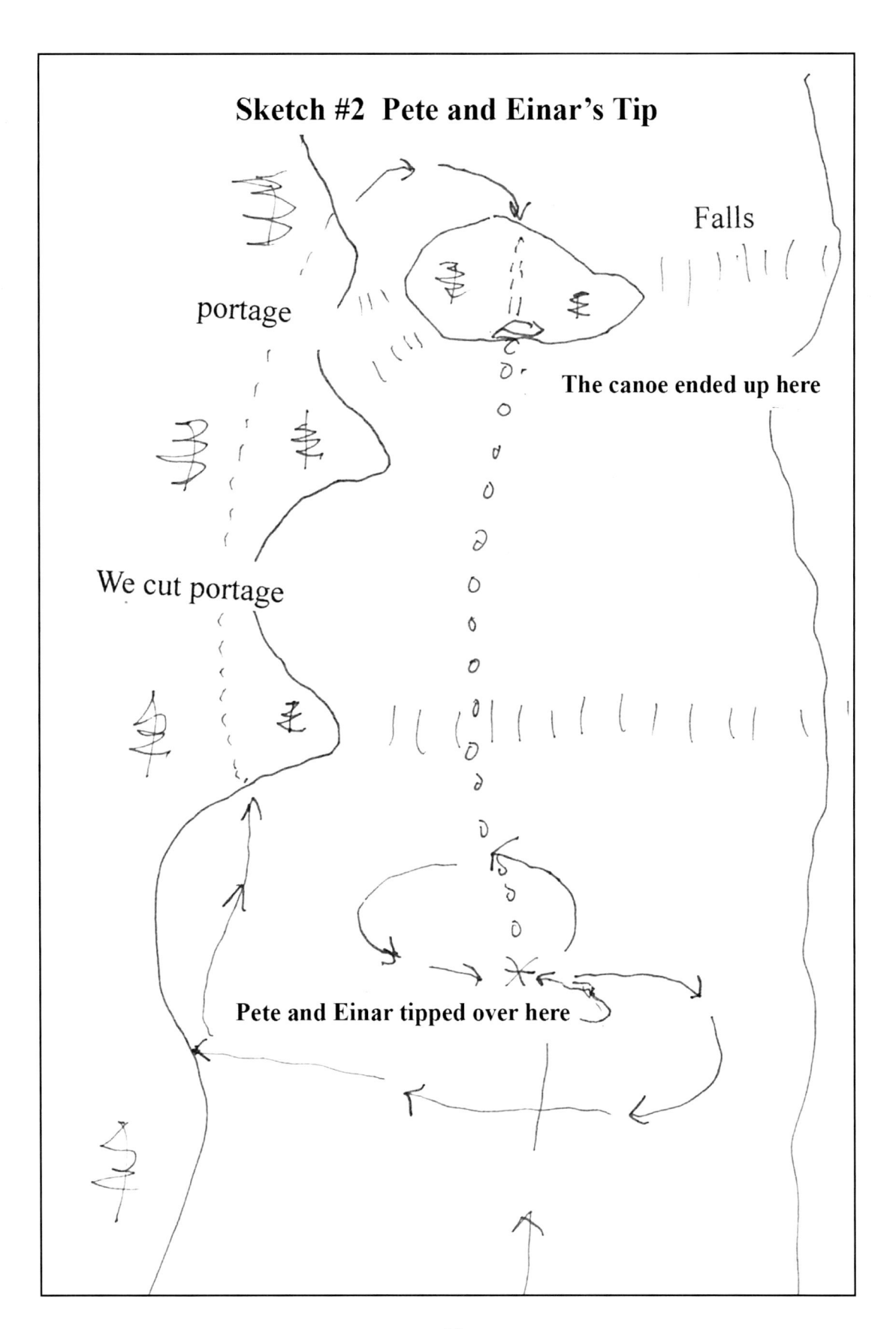

Sketch #2 Pete and Einar's Tip

Falls

portage

The canoe ended up here

We cut portage

Pete and Einar tipped over here

Wally, Terry, Rollie, Bob, and Pete pulled the canoe to shore on the island

pry with and pulling by all of us, we finally got the canoe lose. A few small holes were the only damage and we patched them with some white first aid tape (there was no duct tape at the time). Peter and Einar both lost their old canoeing hats; a small, but not insignificant, loss. (See Sketch #2)

After reloading their canoe, we headed out again and did the rest of Burton Rapids. Now we had the ½ mile Muskeg Portage and Pete and Einar were wet. The Muskeg Portage seemed longer than ½ mile. Pete and Einar seemed on edge after the tip. I think they blamed each other for tipping. The incident had taken a toll on the whole group.

Fortunately, the campsite after the Muskeg Portage was nice. Wally slipped while fishing and was also wet to the waist. I thought maybe he wouldn't snore tonight. Usually when we would go to sleep he would start snoring, I would elbow him real hard and then I would try to go to sleep before he started snoring again.

In the morning it was foggy. Breakfast was trout and walleye with apple compote. The first portage went smoothly on the left just before and around the falls. The next portage was to be a lift-over, but there was no area to lift over as the water was high. We had to cut a track for a portage through some aspens. After a short distance we got back into the river and lined the canoes. From there it was a short ride by canoe to a tough portage with many mosquitoes and rough walking. A little farther on we came to a lift over by the falls. It went well despite the fact that it was wet and slippery.

We came to a temporary fish camp just down river. Fisherman come to the camp by aluminum boats with motors so they very seldom use the portages. We poor people traveling by canoe have to struggle through the brush and aspens. We had lunch there and caught some walleyes and trout. The walleyes liked the Rapala baits but the brook trout hit mostly on small

Sketch # 3 Red Sucker Rapids

Big haystacks but no rocks

Bob and Terry floated down to this point

Two canoes pulled to shore here

Bob and Terry's canoe filled with water

Gods River

Red Sucker River

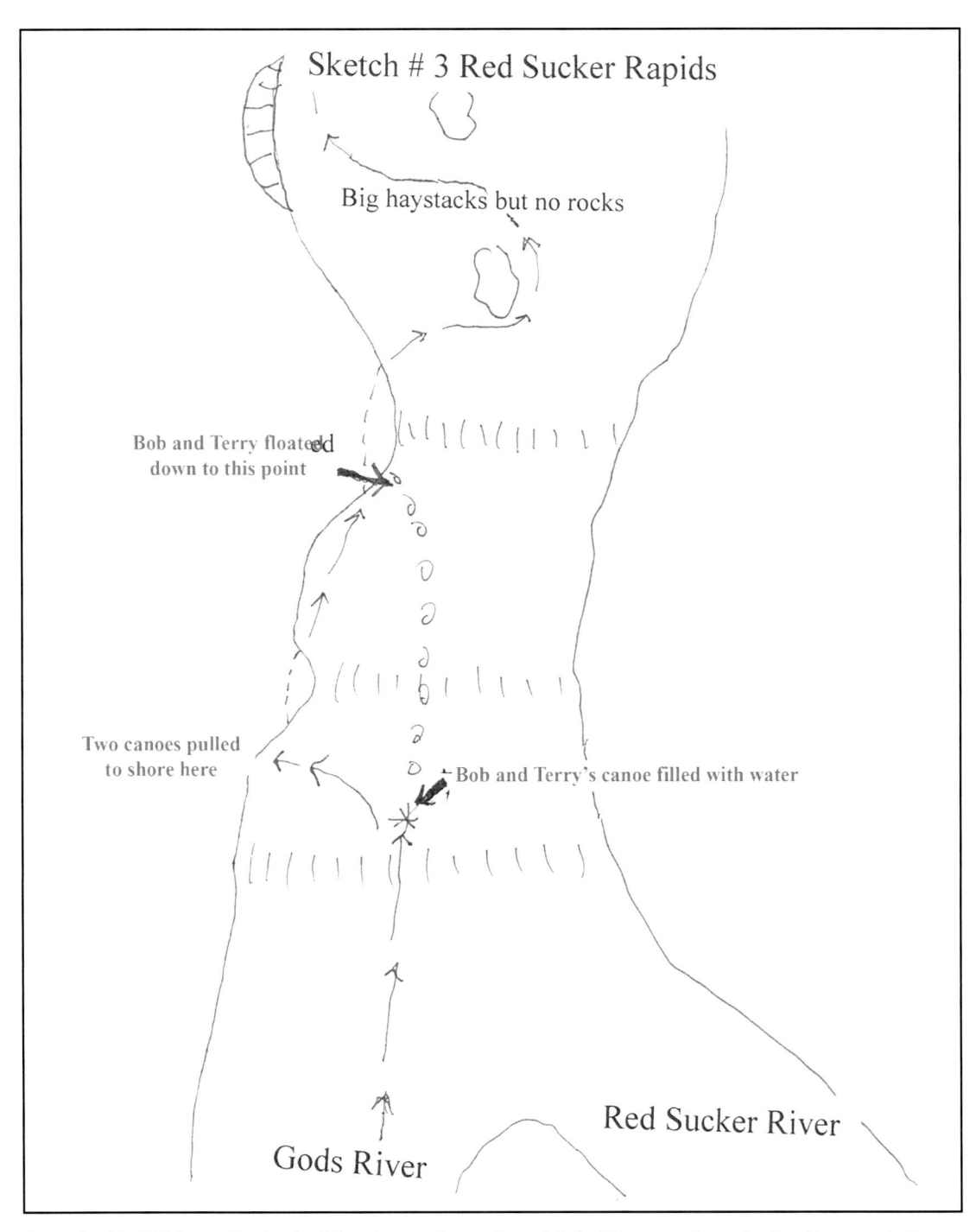

Daredevils. Without the barbed hooks we lost a lot of fish. Then we found a landing net left behind by guests at the camp. From there we made good time until the Red Sucker Rapids.

It was about 6:00 p.m. and we had paddled about 50 miles with a good current. Now we approached the Red Sucker Rapids that we had been warned about. It is at the junction of the Red Sucker River and the Gods River. The Red Sucker comes in from the south. Curt and I led the way. I was in the front, Curt in the back, and Wally in the middle. Terry, who was following, said all of a sudden we dropped out of sight. We were hit by six and seven foot waves close together. With a lot of water in the canoe we pulled to the left shore. We watched as Terry and

Wally, Einar, Curt, and Bob setting up the sail rig

Bob came over the lip of the rapids and tipped over. Bob reminded me later that I yelled "see you at York Factory" as they came floating by us. They rode down with the current over the next section of the rapids straining to hold on to the canoe. Luckily, they were able to keep their grip on the canoe as it protected them from the rocks. The canoe finally stopped up against a sandbar. Pete and Einar came next and made it to where we were. They dumped the water they had taken in their canoe. From there we lined down the left shore and cut some portage on the shore to make it to where Bob and Terry had landed.

They were all right and were tipping the water out of their canoe and ready to go on. We all headed for a small island in the rapids just below a high cliff bank. From there the rapids were full of big haystacks but no rocks. These last rapids went on for about 200 to 300 yards. We were all glad to see the end of the Red Sucker Rapids. We ended up with a lot of water in the canoes, but no red suckers. I commented to Curt that it had been a lot of fun; maybe we should hike back up and try it again. No one agreed. Everyone slept great that night after a 50 mile day of paddling and rapids.

We got up at 6:30 a.m. the next morning for a breakfast of trout and walleye at a beautiful campsite but with poor fishing. After a short distance, the river turned north and we decided to try sailing with the wind on our backs. We tied the three canoes together and cut some poles and put up a tarp for a sail.

With Pete ruddering in the back, we cruised up the river with no padding needed. It went great. We ate our lunch as we moved along the river. About 5:00 p.m. the wind changed and a big dark cloud rolled in. We took down the sail but the canoes were still tied together as we approached the small Indian village of Shamattawa. Now the wind was strong from the north and the river was wider due to the added water from the Shamattawa River. The rain began to pour down on us. The wind and the additional current from the new river caused high waves. With the canoes tied together, and all seven paddling and soaking wet, we crossed the river to the village and pulled up on shore.

There we met Ross and Frazier, Englishmen, who ran the Hudson Bay Store at Shamattawa. Charles Arthurson, the minister of the St. John Anglican Church of Shamattawa also greeted us. Cooking was gratefully done out of the rain in the house where Ross and Frazier lived. We accepted without hesitation, their invitation to sleep on their warm, dry floor. It was good to be out of the cold rain.

When Sevareid and Post arrived at Shamattawa the two Hudson Bay men running the post at Shamattawa at the time, brought them into their cabin and fed them, gave them hot water to wash, etc., and also gave them a place to sleep on the floor.

The men at Shamattawa informed us that an Indian had shot a polar bear the day before we arrived. The next day two Indian boys took us on a tour with the intention of showing us where the polar bear had been shot but they could not find the place.

The Indian women made beadwork and brought samples for us to see. I liked a pair of deerskin moccasins with fur trim, but there was not much beadwork on them. The lady said she had some others with more beadwork. Later she came back with what I think was the same pair of moccasins but with many additional beads. It hadn't taken her long to add the beads and I did buy the moccasins with an even greater appreciation of her talent. Wally bought a dickanocken, a type of baby cradle mothers use to carry infants on their backs.

In the morning the wind was blowing strong from the north and the river did not look like a place we wanted to be. We decided to stay a little longer in Shamattawa. A plane landed which allowed us to send a message to postpone our pickup date at York Factory until Sunday. Charles Arthurson took us on a tour of Shamattawa.

Charles Arthurson in front of a typical log house in Shamattawa.

The log church that Charles built

In 1967, when we were there, the Indians lived in small log cabins but from the photos in Sevareid's book it looks like they lived in teepees in the 1930's when he and Post came through. According to Google there is now an ice road in the winter and so many now live in house trailers. The children go off to Indian school during the school year. There was only an elementary school in Shamattawa when we were there in 1967. Charles showed us the log church he was building. He did most of the work himself and it was about half done.

In 1967 the kids played baseball with no real diamond for a field; just a bat and ball. Many of the men played a game with a big nail stuck in the ground and large washers which they threw at the nail. Scoring was based on ringers or how close they can land the washer to the nail. A little like miniature horseshoes. They seemed to do a lot of gambling on the game. They had a lot of free time with little work available. There was some hunting and guiding in the fall but not much else. Some have trap lines. In the evening we went to the council room to hear fiddle music and see dancing. They liked country music, especially Hank Williams and George Jones.

At 6:30 a.m. the following morning we got up after sleeping on the floor and had eggs and potatoes for breakfast indoors. A real luxurious start to the day. At The Hudson Bay Store I bought a carving knife like the ones used by the Indians in the 1700s. The Hudson Bay Store still stocked them.

Shamattawa is a sad place. The Hudson Bay did not sell raisins and limits the sale of sugar to prevent the making of liquor. In 1980 Eric Sevareid returned to visit Shamattawa and interviewed some nurses in the clinic and they told him they felt isolated with no radio or telephone. Their lives were often threatened by drunken teenagers. They felt sorry for the children who,

Baseball in Shamattawa

down to eight years old, were sniffing gasoline fumes for a high. In 1980 the population was 500. Alcoholism is a big problem.

We headed out about 9:50 a.m. the next morning against a strong wind which forced us to stay close to the west shore. We got to the limestone Rapids about 4:00 p.m.

We were no longer in the Canadian shield country. This is the Shamattawa River and in Cree it means fast running water. The river bottom here is limestone and high clay cliffs line the river on both sides. There are many rocky sections with ridges in the river. The rapids are shallow; we waded and dragged the canoe through many of these sections. In sections in which the water was deeper and fast we climbed back in the canoes and shot the rapids. After the last two miles of rapids we stopped for supper. The flat pieces of limestone made great tables to eat on and then there were many fossils in the limestone that added interest.

After supper we continued on, as the wind had stopped and we made good time. A sandbar was our camp for the night. There were many mosquitoes as always. I woke up about 12:30 a.m. It had cleared up and I stepped outside. The bright colors of the northern lights and the moon were spectacular. It was an amazing sight. I saw the sky up north with all the stars and no human caused light pollution. It reminded me of 1958 when I worked at Loch Lomond Ski Area near Thunder Bay Canada. When we closed after Friday night skiing, the sky was unbelievably clear with bright colors and I enjoyed it while I checked to make sure everyone was off the mountain.

We started the next morning at about 6:00 a.m. in a cold, windy drizzle. After an hour we stopped for a breakfast of porridge. After breakfast we paddled for a long stretch, cold and wet in the rain. A beach looked like a good place to stop but we had a hard time finding any firewood that wasn't wet. We decided to eat some pilot biscuits with honey and go on to the

The crew checking out Limestone Rapids

Pete and Einar wade through with their canoe

junction with the Hayes River. It was a 50 mile day and now the two rivers became one big river.

    Here we found a better campsite but it was still raining. A cold morning and no fishing as the water of the combined rivers was flowing fast and muddy. Everyone was getting tired of the trip and a little on edge. I thought a nice sunny day sure would improve the spirt of us all. Maybe the weather was affected by Hudson Bay which was not too far away. It seemed that Pete and Einar were at each other since their tip in the rapids. I think they blamed each other but had to continue the trip. I heard later that they didn't continue to be best friends after the trip. In Eric's book he tells about how he and Walt got into a real fight, but finally quit when they knew it could end their chance to survive the trip.

    Wally and I had read that Ten Shilling Creek, coming in on the other side of the river, was a good place to fish. The next day the two of us decided to paddle up Ten Shilling Creek and

Upstairs in the York Factory main building

try to catch some trout or walleyes. The rest of the crew were ready to finish the canoeing and decided to go directly to York Factory. Wally and I canoed up Ten Shilling Creek but all we got were jackfish. When we left Ten Shilling Creek we found the river now had big white caps. It was windy and the tide was also affecting the river. It looked threatening but there was an island near where we exited Ten Shilling Creek. I said let's go but Wally said we should stay on the island since we had our tent and a lot of our gear. It would be easier in the morning without the tide. I reminded Wally that the others had the food. It looked like the river was running at maybe 30 MPH. If we tipped, we would end up in Hudson Bay. Wally said "I would prefer Wisconsin to Hudson Bay".

We decided to do it. We crossed the river over to the left side with big waves, wind and whitecaps. The guys saw us coming down along the shore. As we came sailing by they caught the canoe and pulled us up on shore. Maybe you will get us next time, Hudson Bay, but not today.

York Factory was deserted, willow and brush all around the buildings. This was once a seaport in the 1770s with clipper ships bringing in supplies and hauling out furs. York Factory was built in 1684 for the Hudson Bay Company and it was used for more than 270 years. It was named for the Duke of York. In 1686 the French captured forts on James Bay. In 1660, Pierre Le Moyne d'Iberville tried to capture York Factory but was driven away. In 1664, he did capture York Factory and named it Fort Bourbon. The English recaptured it in 1665. In 1697, d'Iberville won the Battle of Hudson Bay and again captured York Factory. It was held by the French until 1713 and was returned to the British in the Treaty of Utrecht. It became the Northern Headquarters of the Hudson Bay Company. As Sevareid and Post arrived at York Factory they saw a schooner at the entrance of the Bay and dogs and Indians interested in who they were. They went to the factors house and were welcomed with food and warmth.

When we arrived the place was abandoned and the main warehouse was in bad shape. Upstairs there were large tables that we thought were used to sort furs. In what had been parade

Wally, Terry and Curt by a canon on the parade grounds

Main building York Factory, 1967

grounds we found a cannon that perhaps had been used by the British or French in their battles. The parade grounds were covered with willows.

In the 1850's there was an extensive trading post and settlement with 50 on site buildings. On the shore where the goods were unloaded we found small musket balls and many things that had been lost from the ships unloading there. Pete found a three inch cannonball. Due to the shallow bottom, seagoing ships anchored at Five Fathom Hole seven miles from the fort. Goods were transferred by smaller boats to the fort. Since our trip the site has been restored. The buildings were closed down in 1957. Since 1968 it has been owned by the Canadian Government and operated by Parks Canada. The Canadian Government provides a caretaker and has restored the buildings. The grounds have been cleared and restored and it is currently an official historical site. Now there are also some part time hunting lodges there.

That night we all had the last bump off of Pete's bottle which was the only one that was not empty. We had a nice supper and got to bed at 10:00 p.m.. They told Wally and me that we were lucky we didn't stay on that island because as they canoed down the river past the island a polar bear was swimming across the river and onto that island. That's as close as I've been to sleeping with a polar bear. I wonder if he would have thought we were food? There were many polar bears in that area and they den there. There are now warnings to canoeists who come here in the summer.

In the morning the Riverton Air flight landed and we pulled the plane close to shore.

Now we could get on board and say goodbye to our canoes. They would remain at York Factory until the winter when the Hudson Bay Company pick them up by snow machine. On the flight out we could see nothing but the wild country below that we had crossed. We landed at Riverton and headed home. Curt, Wally and I returned home to shower and sleep in a comfortable bed for the first time in almost a month.

To finish their trip Sevareid and Post had to portage to the Nelson River from York Factory and then get a ride with Indians up the Nelson River to the railroad. Then they took the train back to Winnipeg. No flight for them in the 1930s.

Pulling the plane closer to the shore.

Chapter Seven: What's Next

It was a busy fall of 1967 selling guitars and amplifiers. My decision to put on country music shows outdoors at Trollhaugen Ski Area the following summer made it even busier. There was lots of work lining up artists and setting up a contract with Trollhaugen for the shows. I had Slim Whitman, Hank Snow, Joe Maphis and Webb Pierce each booked for a weekend. To ease the workload, I hired my friend Steve Peterson to help with the music sales.

In the first part of January, 1968, the Wisconsin Music Educators Convention was held in Madison, Wisconsin. Steve Peterson planned to work southern Wisconsin and meet me in Madison on Thursday night. I would be at the convention site to set up our booth. Steve knew a woman in Madison and thought maybe she could bring a friend and we could all go out Thursday night after the booth was set up. I arranged to meet them at a Mexican Restaurant. We met and although Steve's friend, Martha, did not bring a friend, I joined them anyway. I was impressed by Martha, and she was interested in canoe trips. She had built her own kayak with the help of the Wisconsin Hoofer Club. I thought it was an interesting night, however Martha told me years later she was glad she didn't bring a friend along because she found me obnoxious.

Later in the year Steve moved to Denver and was no longer working for me. When he left I asked him for Martha's phone number. The next time I was in Madison I called her and her roommate said she was skiing in France with a University ski club tour. My interest increased; she's a skier. The next time in Madison we went out. And each time I worked Madison I would see Martha. I met her brother, Chuck, and his wife, Kathy, who were also canoers; they even went canoeing on their honeymoon. I had the opportunity to visit Martha in Whitewater, Wisconsin where I met her parents. Each time we met we talked canoeing.

That summer Wally and I did a canoe trip in the Quetico Park, Manitoba in Canada. He had a friend but I was the lone one in my canoe. I found if I put a large rock on the front seat it was better paddling and I could keep the canoe straight. The problem was carrying the rock over the portages. Then Wally told me to leave the rock and get a new one at the end of the portage. That was much better. I stayed with them for the weekend and then paddled back to the boat landing to return to work.

Martha wanted to do a canoe trip and we thought the Brule River in Northern Wisconsin would be fun. Martha drove her 1966 VW up to Cameron, Wisconsin, where Wally and I met her. We drove to the Brule River for canoeing for the weekend. Martha did fine in the canoe and loved the "Wall" and "Big Joe Rapids," famous rapids on the Brule. Before the trip I had delivered a couple of guitar amps to a county fair where my music dealer had a booth. There was a booth that had Indian arrow points for sale. I bought a couple and had them with me on the trip. When Wally went to town I gave one to the guy at the next campsite and told him to show it to Wally when he came back and ask him about it. When Wally came back Martha and I hid in the tent and listened. Wally was not fooled, he said, "Did Rollie give you this?" Martha and I broke into laughter. You can't fool Wally.

In March of 1969, Bob O'Hara wrote that he and Einar were setting up a Thelon River trip for July. They would take the train to Churchill and fly from there to where the Hanbury River joins the Thelon. Paddle the Thelon to Baker Lake and fly back to Churchill, about 400 miles. Wally and I said we would love to go and that I had a friend, Martha, who would also like to go. We talked to Bob and Einar and they said definitely no women could go on the trip.

Martha dreaming of *The Lonely Land*

    Martha was disappointed. Wally and I thought we could do our own trip with Martha. And Wally would find a canoe partner. We considered the Churchill River based on a reading of the book *The Lonely Land* by Sigurd Olson. Martha was excited about the idea as she was a fan of Sigurd Olson's writings. *The Lonely Land* is the story of Olson's trip with five men across northern Saskatchewan on the Churchill River, a section of the main Voyageur route from Grand Portage on Lake Superior to Fort Chipewyan on Lake Athabasca. *The Lonely Land,* published in 1961 by Alfred A. Knopf Inc., is the story of the well known canoe adventure.

    Sigurd Olson's group started at the south end of Lac Ile a La Crosse but we decided to start at the north end of the lake. We would do a large section described in Olson's book. We let Bob know we were doing our own trip. Wally wrote to Pete Humphrey to see if he could join us and checked with some others but had no luck. So it would be the three of us and we'd require an 18 foot canoe. Because none of us owned one, the decision was made to go through Ely, Minnesota, and rent an 18 foot Grumman canoe from Cliff Wold's Outfitters. We made inquiry about flights into Lake Ile a La Crosse and out from Stanley Mission at the end of the trip. I had only known Martha about a year but I was sure she could handle the Churchill. My thought was this is a brave and adventure loving woman.

    That spring Wally and I spent a weekend in the Boundary Waters Canoe Area. While in Ely, we stopped to see Sigurd Olson at his home. We had a great visit with him and his wife Elizabeth. He shared many interesting details about his experiences on the Churchill and thought we would love the trip. What a wonderful man he was.

    I was in Madison again on business and met Martha to review details of the trip. She would drive up to Center City on Saturday June 28th. Then we would spend Sunday at Wally's packing for the trip. Wally and I had shopped at Hoigards in Minneapolis for freeze dried meals and also some basic groceries. We sealed and labeled food for each day into separate plastic bags. Then we packed them in the food box in the order in which we planned to eat them. Wally had made a food box using thin plywood with shoulder straps on it so it could be portaged. It prevented food from being crushed as could happen if packed in a canvas Duluth Pack. Duluth Packs are designed perfectly for canoe trips in that they nicely fit on the bottom of a canoe. They are difficult for long backpacking trips but OK for portages. We would not take a stove because Wally had a 6" by 16" light weight grill that would fit between two rocks. I provided a small folding army spade so we could dig little latrines at our campsites. We were set to go!

Chapter Eight: On to the Churchill

Martha and I picked up Wally at his home in St. Croix, Wisconsin, on Monday morning, June 30th, at about 11:00 a.m. We loaded all the gear into the back of my three quarter ton Ford pickup. It had a rack on top that could haul an 18 foot canoe. The first time we stopped for gas as we drove north, we discovered the pickup needed three quarts of oil. This was going to be a problem. We couldn't find a place open to work on the truck, so we just added a quart of cheap oil about every 100 miles or so. It became routine to stop for oil and check the gas. In Grand Rapids we stopped to visit with a friend of Wally's. He had hoped to be on the trip with us, but like Pete Humphrey, he could not take off as much time as our trip needed.

The next stop was Cliff Wold's outfitters in Ely, Minnesota, to rent the 18 foot aluminum canoe. With three of us and all our gear for two weeks we would need the longer 18 foot canoe. Cliff was helpful and wished us a safe trip. He cautioned us to be careful with just one canoe and only three people way out in the wilderness without communication with civilization. Cliff also asked if we were sure it would all fit in the canoe.

Ely is one of the main centers for trips into the Boundary Waters of Northern Minnesota. Thousands of canoers leave for canoe trips every summer. Sigurd Olson was one of the main leaders in establishing protection and preserving the Boundary Waters Wilderness Area. There was much opposition initially to setting aside so much area but it has become world famous as a wilderness vacation area.

After tying the canoe onto the pickup we continued on to Detroit Lakes where we stopped for supper. Martha didn't eat much because she was car sick or should I say pickup sick, probably due to the smell of cheap oil burning.

Wally and I drove through the night switching off drivers as we continued northwest. The one not driving lay in the open back of the pickup on a pad in a sleeping bag. The sleeping bag in back was OK but the pickup was bumpy, windy and noisy. Sometimes I thought it was more comfortable to drive than try to sleep in the back.

Arriving in Minot ,North Dakota, Martha, who was feeling better, said that her uncle owned the Ford Garage and Dealership there. That would solve our problem but they were too busy to work on the pickup. Martha took advantage of the opportunity to visit her aunt Ellen who was in the hospital in Minot. While Martha visited her aunt, Wally and I had a big breakfast. Later, the three of us drove on to the Canadian border with the pickup still burning oil.

At the tax free store at the border we bought our supply of rum for the trip. All three of us being a hundred percent Swedish did appreciate a tax free price. We saved some money and that makes any Swede happy.

Now we were in Saskatchewan. When we got to Regina we discovered it was Dominion Day and all the stores were closed. We went on to Prince Albert and the Prince Albert Airport where we were told Jim Money, the contact we had corresponded with about our trip, had left no information. They also had no maps but said we could get some in La Ronge. I assured the people there that we would be in La Ronge in time tomorrow for our flight and they said they would schedule it. We bought some supplies and had a steak dinner at a club with music. The music was good but Wally thought the singer's legs were too skinny for the short skirt she wore.

After driving a hundred miles beyond Prince Albert, we were tired. We hadn't seen any signs of civilization so we simply pulled over to the side of the road and threw our sleeping bags in the back of the pickup. The three of us slept side by side in the pickup bed on this deserted gravel road in rural Saskatchewan. I was wondering what Martha thought of our planning and our accommodations which so far were far less than perfect. The next day, July 2nd, the sun rose bright and fair, we got up early in the back of our pickup, and continued on the gravel road on our way to La Ronge.

La Ronge is a town of about 2,000 people with a seaplane base. We found a garage where we could leave the pickup and have it repaired while we were on our trip. At the seaplane base we talked to the Norcom people and we were extremely frustrated to find that once again they had no information about us or the flight we thought we had scheduled. They promised to find something later in the day for us. When we checked back we found there was a Beaver airplane available at 2:00 p.m. We loaded our gear onto the dock and bought some last minute supplies and, thankfully, the topo maps.

We talked to several people in town to see if we could find someone who had made a similar trip to ours. No one knew anything about that part of the river. It appeared that we were going on a very seldom travelled route. In years past it had been an active route for Voyagers carrying furs and trading goods between Grand Portage on Lake Superior and the large area of what has become northern Canada. At the Hudson Bay Company we bought a few more last minute items. We decided to have a beer and stopped at a local bar. In Saskatchewan at that time, women were not allowed in singles bars. Martha had to go into the family section next door; another unique experience for her. Again, we asked around if there was someone who had canoed the section of the Churchill we were interested in. It was apparently not where the locals went. We decided *The Lonely Land*, the book by Sigurd Olson, would be our best and only guide to for the trip.

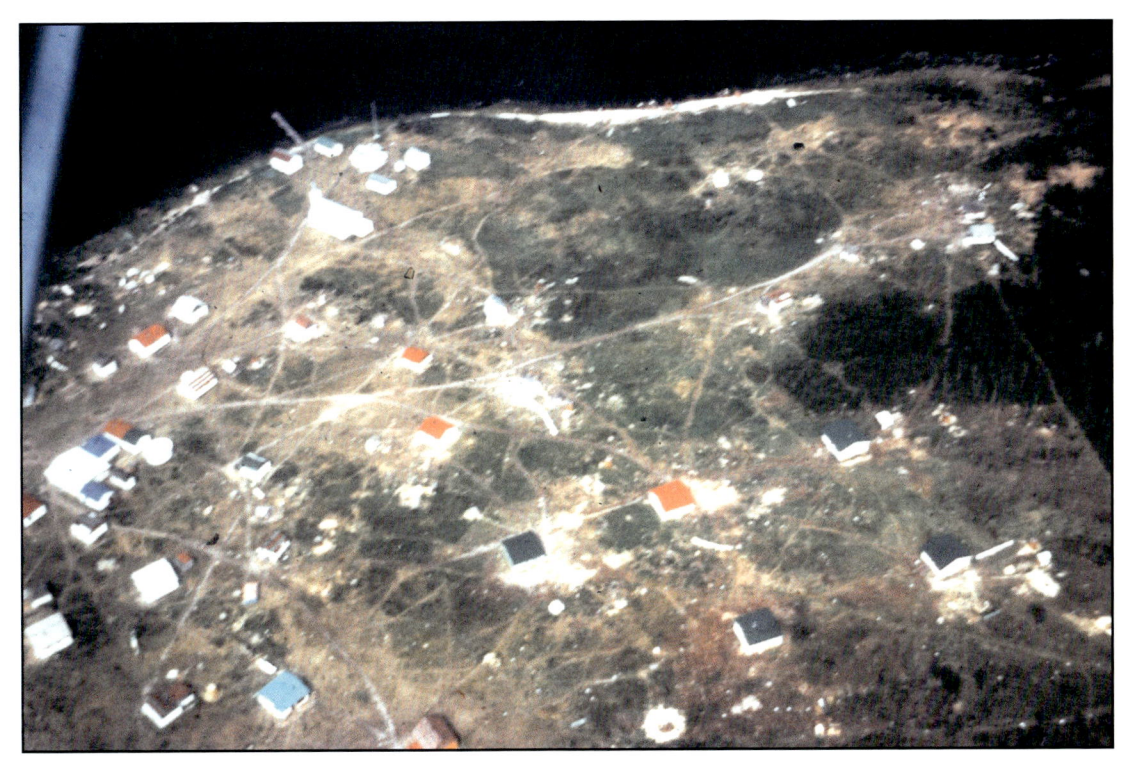

Pinehouse Lake Village

Chapter Nine: On The River

Our flight took off at 2:30 p.m. and was beautiful. It provided us with a bird's eye view of the many lakes, rivers, forests and the few villages. Pinehouse Lake Village was one of those. It was interesting to see the layout of the houses and trails in the village. Since there were no cars, people walked everywhere; no squared off streets or sidewalks; just houses and buildings scattered randomly and paths radiating between them.

After an hour and 20 minutes, we landed on Lake Ile a la Crosse near a small ice dock where ice was harvested in the winter. The canoe was untied from the plane and our gear put on the dock. Now was the time to answer the question we'd been avoiding since leaving Ely: Would it all fit in the canoe? Would there be a place for the third person in the canoe? Was three a crowd in a lonely land?

It was a little lonely and threatening to watch the plane leave and to feel that now we were pretty much alone in the wilds of the north. We were just south of Patuanak, an Indian village mentioned by Olson in his book. The water was slightly fast on the way to the village but it gave us an opportunity to warm up our canoeing skills. (See Map 2)

Sigurd's group had talked about stopping at Patuanak. They did stop briefly, but there were so many dogs, they decided not to camp at the village. We decided to stop and pick up some eggs, bacon, and margarine at the Hudson Bay Store in Patuanak in order to have a first class breakfast the first morning on the river. The village was clearly bigger than the village described by Sigurd. It had both a Hudson Bay Store and a Co-op Store and still had a lot of dogs. It has

Wally says goodbye to our way home if we changed our minds

continued to grow since our visit there; in 1977 a road was made to Patuanak and in 1999 the school was enlarged to grade twelve. It is no longer such a lonely place.

After our visit we headed on hoping for a nice campsite for our first night on the Churchill. All of the area near the village was fairly swampy. After paddling six miles we came to a flat rock shelf that looked like a perfect spot to camp for the night.

It had been a long day of travel by truck, plane and canoe; we slept well for eight hours that night. July third and the morning dawned sunny and warm with a breakfast of bacon and eggs. The confusions and hassles of our travels on the way out were forgotten and we settled into canoeing on the river. As we traveled that day we saw a huge black cross on Cross Island. We paddled on the right side of the island to get a better look at it. It was built to honor someone by the name of Gilbert who had been involved with Indian battles. We later learned the Oblate missionaries from Lac Ile La Crosse had moved there because of the rebellion of 1885. Father Moraud had erected a wooden cross that was later replaced by the iron one.

Wally was not feeling well that first day but as we floated along he seemed to get better. This was a worry as Wally was 61 years old. The canoeing went well and soon we could hear the roar of the Drum Rapids. The rapids gets its name from the roar. The river makes a sharp bend and there was suppose to be a portage across the bend, but there was no sign of it that we could see. We chose to run them.

Now we got into our first real rapids of the trip and we would know many more before the trip is over. The first two sections went smoothly, Wally in front and me in the stern. When we came to the next section we stopped and looked it over. Although the rapids looked OK on the left side and we believed we could make it, there were some bad looking spots. Since it was our first day out, we lined the canoe down the right side. It went quite well, except we got our feet wet. To line a canoe you walk along the shore or just in the water's edge with a rope tied to the front and another tied to the back. The canoe did catch a few rocks as we pulled it through, but we didn't have to unload the canoe and carry our packs and the canoe. Later in the 1990's a cross was erected to warn canoers of the danger of these rapids.

We approached the next rapids and decided to run it with me in the front and Wally in the back. It was going great until I saw a large rock on the right and I yelled, "Go left, Wally". He thought I meant that the rock was on the left and he pulled right which made the canoe go sideways in the current. Fortunately we floated over any rocks and came out without a rock catching and tipping us over. Now I wondered if Martha thought "What have I gotten myself into!" but there was no turning back at this point and we did improve as we went along.

Next came the Leaf Rapids and a choice of a portage on the south side that we could not find, or line the canoe on south shore, or run them with Wally in the stern and me the in the front. We decided to go for it. It was a thrilling ride with rough water and rocks but we sailed through with the canoe talking in just a little water. One of our last minute purchases at the Hudson Bay Store in Patuanak was a Yacht Mop. Now we had a chance to discover how useful it would be get water out of the canoe without having to unload it and tip the water out.

Deer Rapids came next. They were fast, but smooth, on the right side. When there is fast water in the rapids you can slip right through by following the Vs pointing downstream in the current. Rocks are usually a problem when you can't see them because they are below the surface of the water. The downward point Vs clearly direct the way around the unseen rocks.

We stopped for lunch after the first section. Just when we were ready for the second section of the Deer Rapids an Indian motorboat came by and headed right down through the rapids. We just followed their route because they seemed to know the best way through the lower Deer Rapids; it probably wasn't their first time through. We went down just as smoothly as they did.

We camped for the night next to the Dipper Rapids. The campsite by the rapids was a beautiful spot on a big flat rock. Southern Saskatchewan was mostly grassland but the northern part of the state is rock of the Canadian Shield Plateau. So we were now entering Canadian Shield country, campsites from here on should be good, something we had learned in The Boundary Waters canoe area in Minnesota.

We met a couple of men who were building a water gauge for the Canadian water service. They camped on the other side of the river and we had a conversation. They said ours was quite the adventure with just two men, one woman and one canoe. What did they mean by that? We

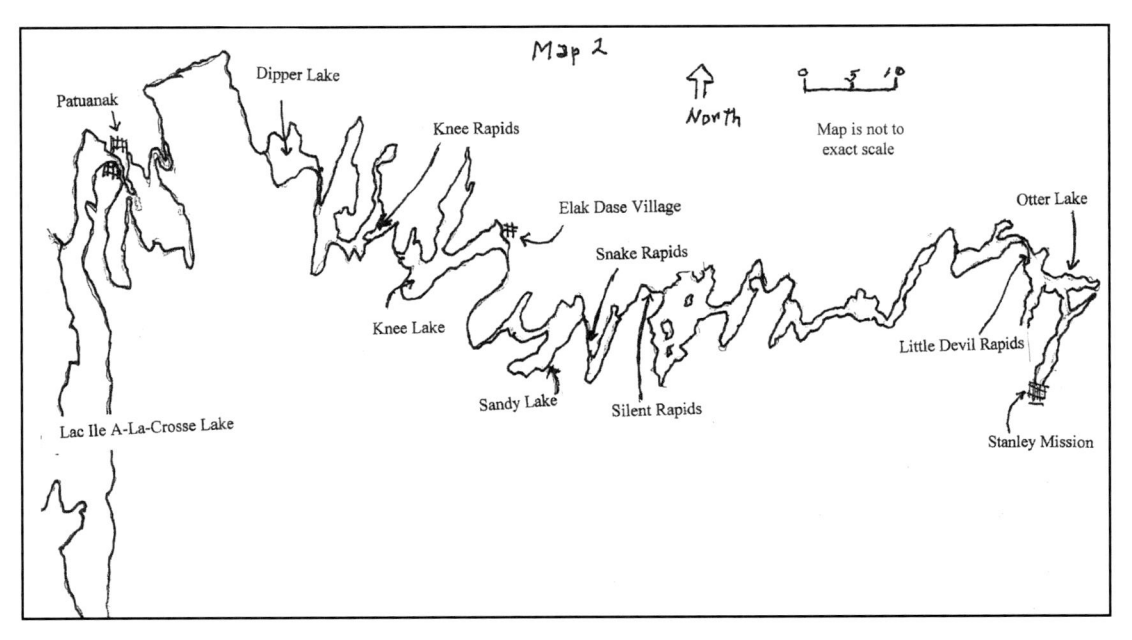

Wally pushing and Rollie keeping the canoe on the track.

said we're eager to try it and hoped we would make it. We enjoyed the site and had a delicious supper. While washing dishes I leaned over the fast water and my sunglasses fell off. They were long gone with a lot of hopefully sunny days to follow. During the night the sound of the rapids reminded me of air conditioners and lulled me to sleep.

The next morning we started across Dipper Lake on another beautiful clear blue day. The night before Martha had complained "Don't I ever get the chance to paddle?". So Martha got her chance to paddle. Dipper Lake is a good sized lake and less than halfway across clouds came in and the wind blew in our faces. Wally was in back and Martha was in the bow. As they paddled on against the wind and big waves, I had to quote an old voyager rhyme in voyager accent "Da vind et blows on lac st clare et blows den blows some more. If you don van to drown on dat big lac yu best stay close to shore".

At the far side of Dipper Lake after a long, hard paddle, we gratefully stopped for lunch on a shield rock. Martha seemed to have enjoyed the paddling, but was content to be the duffer, the one in the middle of the canoe not paddling, for the afternoon. The campsite that night was again on typical Canadian shield. We caught walleyes for supper. There was total agreement that the walleyes of the north are the best tasting fish and the campsites are the most beautiful.

Our campsite was near the beginning of a portage. In the morning we found that the portage had an old wooden rail track and a cart to roll canoes and boats across the portage. The rail and the cart were in bad shape but looked usable. After breakfast we put our canoe on the cart, loaded our gear into the canoe and rolled it across the portage. Reportedly this rail and cart has been upgraded a number of time since our trip.

The cart came off the track a few times but we persisted. It was much easier then carrying the canoe and the gear across the portage. Once we got back on the water the wind was blowing. Martha was eager to be in front again, Wally was in the back and I was duffing in the middle. As a big wave went by, I had to recite this old saying to them: "Captain, Captain the ship is sinking! Whatever shall we do?" Captain replied, "Well throw out the anchor." "But, Captain, the anchor has no chain!" The Captain said, "Well throw it out anyway, it might do some good." After that, each time anyone suggested a questionable solution to a problem we said, "Well do it anyway, it may do some good".

Wally and Martha kept us out of the wind by hugging the leeward side of the many islands we passed. We stopped for lunch on a smooth rock where we were impressed by the striations left by glaciers. This is great shield country and the rocky shore makes for nice camping. We fished a while but caught only northerns (jackfish). Martha had a walleye on her line but it got away. Wally and I paddled the rest of the day.

Later that afternoon, we stopped at a small Indian settlement near Primeau Lake. The Indians don't see many non-Indians travel past in a canoe without a motor. A few children and an old grandma with no teeth were watching us as we pulled up. The children were happy to share some of our candy. This village was inhabited only in the summer. The only buildings were a couple of cabins and a church. While we enjoyed the lack of civilization for a few weeks in the wilderness, we were struck by what a completely different life these Indians lived compared to our own lives.

We went on and found a high rock shelf to camp for the night. Just before the campsite we saw an island full of American White Pelicans. Unfortunately they flew before we could paddle close enough to take pictures but left us with awesome pictures in our minds of the large white birds with their black wing tips rising together against the bright blue sky.

The walleyes we caught for supper offered a welcome addition to our usual freeze dried meals. At supper each night Wally would say to Martha, "You're the best looking woman

I scratch my head as I think I see a way through

Rollie and Wally tipping out the water

I've seen all day". Tonight, after stopping at the Indian village Wally said, "Martha you're the second best looking woman I've seen all day". That night we had a beautiful sunset and we decided that it was our own Fourth of July fireworks. Just after supper a nighthawk landed at our site and Wally, feeling lonesome, invited it to join him for the night but it flew away.

July 5th, dawned another beautiful day, with no mosquitoes or blackflies since we were on a flat rock ledge, with firewood and few mosquitoes. We started the day with breakfast and a drink of hot buttered rum with maple syrup, brown sugar, and butter. At the end of the lake we came to Crooked Rapids. Here the river goes north at the first, not so difficult, section of rapids then turns east with a rough section of rapids; and then south with an easier last section. There is a portage reportedly on the right that cuts across the point. Like so many others, it is no longer used and as a result it was difficult to find. We decided we could run the first section. The right side of the rapids looked the best. I thought we could do it with me in the back and Martha in the front for her first time paddling in the rapids. We took them beautifully according to Wally. Now Martha was paddling the front in the rapids. What a woman! The next part looked bad and perhaps it should be portaged. But I thought we could go down the middle with Wally in the front and me in the stern.

It was going fine until about half way I thought, "What are we doing in this canoe in these rapids when we could be safe on the portage?" Suddenly we dropped off some small falls and the bow went under a wave taking in a heavy slosh of water. There were four and five foot waves on both sides. A second wave added to the already heavy canoe. Now we had six to eight inches of water in the canoe. Canoes are not built to float and cannot be easily steered when carrying three passengers, all their gear for two weeks, and the weight of almost eight inches of water. Wally continued to paddle as straight and hard as he could to keep up enough speed so I

Rollie portaging

could steer from the back. I worked hard to keep us in line with the current. Keeping the canoe straight with the current was of utmost importance as any move across the current would surely tip us. We stayed to the left of a small rocky island and crashed through several more huge waves. The water smoothed out a bit and we realized we had made it through the worst of the Crooked Rapids. Carefully we pulled to shore to breathe a sigh of relief and empty the canoe. The packs were a little wet but they had heavy plastic bag liners in them.

At the lower end of the rapids we saw the pink granite rock shelf that is mentioned in *The Lonely Land*. He and his crew had camped on that shelf on their trip. Had we checked earlier in our copy of *The Lonely Land,* we would have read that they were warned about Crooked Rapids by an Indian who told them that it's a bad one. We had a fun ride through the last section of the Crooked Rapids without even looking them over before we went down. We easily dodged rocks on left side, then crossed smoothly over to the other side and out at the bottom.

A little farther where the river turns east, we came to Knee Rapids where we decided to land on the left shore to reconnoiter. Martha and I walked down to check them over. While we were looking at the rapids and falls we found a little used portage of about a quarter mile on the north side of the river. It was probably an old Voyageur trail. The Indians today, with their aluminum boats and motors, have no need to portage; they just run the rapids without worry or stopping. If you don't need to portage you don't need to unload or carry and you save a great deal of time and effort. This portage was rough as it was on a steep hillside and apparently had not been used in a long time. Nevertheless, it was better than going over the falls. I picked up the canoe to portage and thought "This is no 17 foot canoe". The extra weight and length of the 18 footer on my shoulders was challenging. As I maneuvered around the grown trees on an angled slope. A tough portage and I was glad it was not too long and that I didn't slip down the side of the bank.

Martha lands a nice jackfish

At the end of the portage we found a deep hole below the small falls. It was a fishing paradise, we caught one northern after another.

At one time we all three had 20 pound northerns on our lines. Several of the casts brought in walleyes which we kept for supper. We had pinched the barbs on our hooks so we could release the northerns and the extra walleyes. On the high hill across the river from us we spotted a bald eagle nest with two eaglets in it. One of the adult eagles flew over us again and again as if to check us out. This pristine stop along the river made it clear to us why we braved the rapids and struggled against the wind just to be here.

That night we camped on a small island across from the entrance to Knee Lake. There were no mosquitoes and no black flies at that campsite high on the shelf overlooking the lake. In this lovely evening we had a toast of rum for a great day of wild rapids and exceptional fishing. The walleyes were delicious and were about all we ate that night. The sunset lit up the western sky; several forest fires in the area added to the remarkable reds and oranges in the sky.

July 6th; we start the morning with eggs and bacon. Wally and Martha paddled across Knee Lake.

On calm sections of water the front and back paddlers switch paddling sides at the same time to maintain a balance in stroking. The switch occurs at the command of the paddler in the stern. The stern paddler says "hut" and both switch sides by bringing the paddle over head to the other side. This worked well except when the front paddler was lost in the scenery or in a wilderness induced trance. The "huts" from the back were then frequently missed. It didn't take long until we came up with lots of "hut" related foolishness. Like, "Look at that hut over there" or "Why do football players say hut". Sometimes a "hut" would appear randomly somewhere in

We came to Elak Dose Village and visited the Father Moraud Church

Father Moraud's church

the sentence: "That sure was good fishing hut back there". We came up with a wide variety of disguised "huts" in an attempt to catch the forward paddler. Once when paddling in the front, I completely broke the peacefulness of the wilderness by screaming and throwing the paddle into the air when the person in back said "hut". A little foolishness and it's no longer boring in the calm of another beautiful lake.

We had started before the wind got strong and would push against us again. About half way across Knee Lake the wind picked up at the entrance to Bentley Bay. Martha gave up her paddle to me and Wally and I fought our way against the wind and waves for several hours. We stopped for lunch and after that Martha returned to paddling.

Next we came to Elak Dose Village where we visited the church that Father Moraud built. The psalm books and the hymnals were in Cree. We did not see any adult Indians but the children came for candy and pictures. They go off to school in Lac Ile La Crosse in the fall but return to the village for the summer. We noticed fishnets set along the shore. In Olson's *The Lonely Land*, he tells of meeting Father Moraud there (in a freighter canoe). He had lived in the north country for 40 years as a priest to the Indians.

From here the current was good and the wind was at our back. We set up camp about 7:30 p.m. after a hard day mostly paddling into the wind. Our camp was on a rock ledge with lots of firewood. Because we were on a shield rock with a slight breeze, there were not many black flies or mosquitoes,

We had now reached the lower part of Haultain Marsh. We caught some northerns and released them. Martha made a good bannock which we had with spaghetti for supper. A flock of 25 pelicans flew over and there were many ducks and shorebirds in the marsh area. The three of us were tired after ten hours and 35 miles against the wind. A hot cherry drink with rum sent us to bed. The Bourgeois (Wally) let us sleep in the next morning. The old Bourgeois of voyageur days was the accepted leader and would not have been so nice. I don't know if Sigurd, the Bourgeois in *The Lonely Land,* would let his crew sleep in but we deserved and appreciated a late start this morning.

In the Haultain area we saw lots of terns. It started with saying "Wally is that your tern." From then on we entertained ourselves with tern stories. Another one I remember is, a German brought this bird into a butcher shop and wanted to get a sausage so the butcher took a tern for the wurst. The stories got even wurst.

On July 7th we woke up to a cloudy day. We thought it was OK to be out of the sun as we were getting sunburned. It was a slow start when we broke camp. I pushed off into the channel and into the wind with Martha in the front. After we crossed Dreger Lake we came to small rapids which we shot. At our lunch stop Wally tried fishing again and caught a northern on almost every cast but no walleyes. Then we fought the wind across Sandy Lake to Snake Rapids. After walking up the left side of the river to reconnoiter Snake Rapids we decided to take the chance and run them.

This would be our biggest rapids. It was one that Sigurd and his crew portaged around because they found a well-used portage. We found none. The route we choose would work if we hit it just right or it could be big trouble for us. It reminded me of studying a slalom ski race course and trying to remember it as you skied down the slope. In a ski race you only have a slower time if you missed the line you planned to take. If we missed our line in the canoe, we could get wet or worse.

Wally took the bow and I took the stern. There were boulders on the left and huge haystacks on the right of our planned route. We would go down the middle. In *The Lonely Land,* Sigurd called these haystacks pinwheel spouts that could flip a canoe over like a top. Our planned route would be to go upstream a little, turn down the middle, then work to the left and follow the main current down between the rocks on the left and the haystacks on the right. The roar of the rapids and the view ahead looked scary but we were on our way. As we turned down our route I said softly "Wally give us some power now and we will go left" he gave me power and we hit our planned line just right. The wall of water on the right was huge and we missed the rocks on the left. Martha cheered as we pulled out at the bottom. I think we had impressed her. I thought Martha was brave to take a chance with these rapids, rapids that would scare many people, and then grin like, "Wow, what an adventure."

Then the rain started. I thought I'll see how Martha likes camping in the rain. We were all so thrilled by our fine rapids run that we didn't mind a little rain. There was a camping spot before the next section of rapids so we pitched our tents and put up a tarp over an area to have a fire out of the rain. The river was close enough that we could fish from under the tarp. The campsite was on a narrow island and we were able to catch a few walleyes, caught mostly by Martha. I remembered a comment made by Faucet, the great Amazon explorer, as he reminisced about a trip, "One only knows a man well when in the wild with him." I had traveled with Wally in the wilderness many times and knew him well. I think I was also beginning to know Martha.

We looked over the next days rapids and decided to portage the packs since they were already unloaded and run the rapids with an empty canoe. We had had a little water in the tents from the rain but not bad. Wally had a roaring fire going by the time the rest of us were up and we had hot buttered rum. It was still raining so we decided to stay and fish. Wally fished upstream and I fished downstream while Martha made breakfast. We caught enough walleyes for lunch, however it seemed that we had to catch four northerns for each walleye.

We changed our minds about the rapids and decided to portage the canoe as well as the packs, and not run the rapids. I like to hum or sing when I work, ski, or do portages. On this long portage I thought of a tune from the musical "Carousel". So I hummed "when you walk down a portage keep your canoe held high, and don't be afraid of the bears, at the end of the portage is a golden sky and a lake waiting for your canoe" or "at the end is the sweet vocal call of the loon."

The last part of the Snake Rapids we ran without stopping to reconnoiter. Wally was in the stern, I was in the bow. He directed to go left or go right and we rode down smoothly without even coming close to a rock.

We were surprised to see a helicopter fly over, which we guessed was prospectors from a mining company. The paddle across MacDonald Bay was easy as the wind was with us. In the narrows between Snake Rapids and McDonald Bay we saw the pictographs Sigurd had mentioned in *The Lonely Land*. It was interesting to stop and investigate. Next was Pinehouse Lake, past Cow Park island, and on to a pleasant campsite on an island.

The tents were still wet, so we set them up to dry out. After supper we built a big fire and dried things out. That evening the loons were extra persistent in calling; we assumed they wanted to share some brandy with us. It was early still, so we washed our clothes. In the morning we were awakened by loud shouts from Wally jumping into the cold water for a swim. Martha and I joined him but none of us were in the water long. I hated to leave this beautiful campsite.

Do we take this on the right, left, or down the middle?

    Martha and I paddled across Pinehouse Lake with a brisk wind on our backs. After lunch we started across Sandfly Lake with Wally in the stern and me in the bow. This area turned out to be the most scenic so far. We crossed Sandfly in two hours with big rollers pushing us along. When we landed to the right of the outlet of Sandfly Lake the rollers were following us so we pulled the canoe up the shore as fast as we could and only got a little water in canoe.

    After we mopped out the bottom of the canoe we walked down to check out Needle Rapids. We decided to run the first part but needed to make a hard left turn at the start to avoid the four and five foot horses, then stay left all the way to avoid additional horses. Everything was lashed in and Wally was in the stern and I was in the bow. We came around the corner but couldn't get as far left as we had planned to keep the canoe from the going sideways. The first huge wave caught us and gallons of water poured in. Now we were in the middle and hoping we could keep the canoe straight and with the current. Big wild horses crashed on us with Wally on his knees in eight inches of water in the back, grunting and panting, but he held us on course and we pulled to shore at the bottom. We were laughing at Wally asking what sounds he was making and we wanted to know if he was having a heart attack. Not a joke in the wilderness. I think we laughed to deny how worried we were.

    After loading up the canoe again we found an island in the middle of the next set of rapids. Either side looked tough. Sigurd's crew portaged over the middle of the little island. We later learned they were class three rapids.

    As we walked down the right side and looked at the left side it looked pretty wild. Trying to pick a safe route, it seemed barely possible to run. If we made the right turns at the right time we could do it. There were seven big spouts and I thought OK, let's try. After another check we decided let's go, with me in the back and Wally in the front. It started with a three foot drop and before we could get set a big wave crashed over us. Again, we were shooting through wild water with fast moving waves and a load of water in the canoe. My arms hurt as I worked to keep us straight and Wally kept adding power to keep our speed as fast as the current. And again we made it; exhausted, but excited, we paddled up to a flat rock to empty the canoe.

After a mile we came to Needle Falls. The portage on the right had many aspen cut as poles laid crossways on the path so you could pull your canoe over to the other side without unloading the gear. The poles rolled a little as we pulled the canoe, me pulling on the rope in front and Wally and Martha pushing in back. Because it was a falls, the portage was still used and not grown over. I walked over to view the falls and there was a pelican by the falls, I think he was looking for fish.

I found a pair of sunglasses. I had lost mine while bending over the river to wash dishes on one of the first days of the trip. Now I had a replacement pair. I used them after the trip when I traveled. I found I was getting headaches from them and discovered they were prescription.

We paddled on near Silent Rapids and found a beautiful campsite on a high rock ledge. We always looked for these rocky open areas to keep away from mosquitoes and blackflies. After the tents were up we toasted the two rapids we just barely survived. Supper was beef stroganoff and banana pudding. At 10:00 p.m. we went to bed after a 30 mile day and another great sunset.

On the 9th day out we were all in high spirits. The trip hadn't been rough enough to stress any of us out. Maybe that would change if the weather turned bad or the portages got longer. Wally and Martha took the canoe out in the morning to take a picture of our great campsite while I fixed the coffee, bacon and pancakes for breakfast. After breaking camp Wally and I paddled a couple hours to Silent Rapids. At a flat rock we stopped and caught a couple walleyes for supper. We caught both northerns and walleyes but Martha caught the walleyes, what

Wally thought, "What's the deal!" I think we missed our route

a woman. Martha and Wally paddled through Silent Rapids. In *The Lonely Land,* Sigurd quotes Alexander Mackenzie saying that the rapid "qui ne parle point", or the rapids that never speak. The rapids are very dangerous with powerful whirlpools that should be avoided. We found the Silent Rapids to be mostly fast water due to the high water level.

We paddled on to a rock ledge on Black Bear Island Lake for lunch. Lunch was usually pilot biscuits, cheddar cheese, lemonade, beef jerky and a chocolate bar. Bear Island Lake is covered with islands and if you ever saw the old Hamm's Beer ads it looked just as beautiful. The islands had stands of mature spruce with some aspen and the sky had high feathery clouds. At each bay we would be greeted by the singing of a loon. As we canoed Martha was reading aloud from Sigurd Olson's "The Lonely Land". It provided a perfect narration for the world we were paddling through. Canoeing across Black Bear Island Lake required close concentration. There are so many inlets and islands and bays that it is difficult to match those around you with the map. You could enter a bay that has no outlet or head down an inlet that goes nowhere. It's essential to know which island or bay or inlet you are near and to be on the right route in order to exit the lake at the Churchill River outlet.

I kept the map on my lap to be sure we're on the right side of islands and in the right bay. There's only one way out of the lake and if you don't locate the exit from the lake you can spend days trying to find your way out. Black Bear Island is a big lake so we paddled until we were tired. Martha said she was amazed at our strength and endurance as we paddled and she sat in the middle seat listening to the steady swish of the paddles and the even huts.

Wally and I paddled until 8:00 p.m. and finally stopped at a nice campsite on an island with lots of firewood. We fished and caught a couple northerns. Then Martha walked over to a rocky area that I said would not be good for fishing and she landed two walleyes. I made a delicious bannock (camp bread) with cheese. Later I saw Wally throw a piece of the crust into the fire. I was not happy and let him know it was wonderful bannock and you shouldn't throw any of it away. We fried the walleyes breaded with pancake mix in margarine. They were golden brown and delicious and maybe even better than the bannock crust Wally threw away.

In the evening our nightcap was the last of our vodka. We used the same plastic bottles for water, lemonade and vodka. Earlier Martha had used a bottle she thought was water to make lemonade, without realizing it was the vodka bottle. She added the lemonade mix and shook it up. Then took a big swig and said "Wow, not your normal lemonade!" After that the vodka had a unique flavor.

Our weather had been fair with only one rainy day so far, and few mosquitoes and blackflies. No wonder our spirits were high. On July 11th we woke at 6:00 a.m.; it was sunny with a slight breeze from the east. Breakfast was a bowl of Red River Cereal and fruit with leftover bannock and walleye from the night before, giving us a good start for a long day. We crossed the rest of Black Bear Island Lake and the narrows to Birch Rapids Portage. It was on the right side and about a quarter of a mile long, but well traveled and cleared. I portaged the canoe and the food pack that was not so heavy now. Lunch was at the beginning of Trout Lake. Martha and Wally paddled the whole length of Trout Lake with a strong tail wind. At Trout Falls we had a tough portage on the right side with a steep hill that was not cleared very well. I had a tough time carrying the 18 foot canoe between the narrowly spaced trees and across a rocky and slippery side hill with many deadfalls lying on the trail. At the far end we fished. I caught walleyes for supper in the half hour rest after the tough portage.

Martha and I ran the next rapids. After winding our way down the narrows we went over a short drop with just a little water coming in although we still got wet. We did a short portage across a narrow point. Then we crossed a small lake and ran Little Rock Rapids with Wally in the stern. It went well with a sharp turn to miss some huge wild horses. Next we had a long, tough portage of half a mile past the lower Little Rock Rapids. We no more than got into the canoes and it started raining. Now things were getting tougher. To add to the fun, a thunderstorm drenched and worried us as we shot across the lake to where we made camp on a rock ledge connecting two islands. In Martha's log she wrote, "Now I've had it, my legs are too tired and my pack is too heavy and I don't want any part of it any more."

Later that evening the sky cleared and a wonderful rainbow filled the sky. After a hot drink and three walleyes for supper around a nice warm fire, Martha was happy and dry again. Spirits lifted with the prospect of sleeping in a tent on deep moss and tall old spruce trees all around. You could hear the soft whisper of the last rapids behind us. Our travel for the day was about 31 miles with four portages and some good rapids.

We woke to find a clear sky and no wind. Breakfast was Red River cereal and the last of the bacon. As we were ready to go a boat pulled in near our campsite to fish. They were the first people we had seen in five days. It was a guide with a couple from Chicago doing some fishing. Looks like we are getting near civilization. They were staying on Mcintosh Lake, at the Sportsman's Lodge.

After a little paddling, we came to narrows with two small rapids. The first one put a little water in the canoe but the second rapids we ran like pros. Wally and I paddled the first part of Dead Lake (Nipew Lake) before breaking for lunch. Martha and Wally paddled couple of hours after lunch. They made good time with the wind on their backs. Wally and I then paddled while Martha rested and caught some rays. The country continues to be beautiful with mostly spruce forests lining the waterways. There was evidence of a big forest fire burn on Dead Lake. We began to notice more people and a few cabins as we came closer to civilization. We had paddled about 30 miles since breakfast and arrived at the Great Devil Rapids portage in late afternoon.

At Great Devil Rapids portage it began to rain. The mile-long portage looked well-used so we didn't bother to reconnoiter the rapids but just headed off in the rain. I carried the canoe and the others each had a pack. The portage had a welcome rest stop halfway where I could rest the canoe on a branch but wouldn't have to set it down and pick it up again. We did the portage in an hour and 45 minutes. The rain made the packs wet and heavy. The canoe, however, doesn't get any heavier in the rain and with it over my head it served as a huge umbrella. We wore rain suits on the portage which makes walking harder and the loads feel heavier. There were a lot of bugs here; I think because we were nearer people.

After this portage we paddled a short distance and came to the Little Devil Rapids Portage which was less than half a mile. We took the portage for the first part of the Little Devil then came to a fork which gave us the option to continue on the portage or go to the river and run the rest of the Little Devil. The name gave us confidence and the weather had finally cleared. We decided to run that little devil.

Chapter Ten: The Mean Little Devil

The last part of Little Devil looked runnable so we threw the packs in the canoe and, for the first time on the trip, did not tie them in. With Wally in the back and me in the front we made the first two shoots and the turn just fine. After the turn, we saw a sudden drop over a ledge just ahead. It stretched across the entire river. We had no choice but to take it. Wally picked a spot that seemed to have the most water going over it, but it was not enough. We hung up on the ledge and Wally stepped out to try to push us off the ledge. He stepped into a deep hole and ended up under the canoe pulling it over on top of him and dumping Martha, me, packs and all into the river. We all knew it was foolish to ever go into the rapids without taking the time to tie in the gear, especially with only one canoe and no back up of any kind. But we had just come from the portage and Little Devil looked easy. So now we had gear floating in the river and the canoe wedged against a rock ledge. We were wading in waist deep rushing water with a slippery bottom trying to grab our gear. This we knew was serious trouble. A large flat rock was near us and near the shore. Struggling against the current in wet clothes we managed to pull most of our soaking, heavy bags of gear over onto the rock or to drag it back into the canoe and tie it in. Once we were sure we wouldn't lose any gear down the rapids, it was time to try to save the canoe. The canoe, with the water rushing in, seemed to be bending a little so we had to get it loose and hold on to it so it would not go on down the river. With all three of us wet and cold we pulled and pushed until we finally got the canoe lose and over to the flat rock with the gear. We unloaded the gear and laid it out to dry. Wally's hat and paddle were the only things that had floated down the river. I put the now empty canoe in the water and paddled down to the backwater where these two items stopped and brought them back. Fortunately the Duluth Packs and food box were lined with heavy plastic pack bags so most of the stuff stayed dry. A couple of powerboats came up the rapids on their way to check their bear snares. They checked to see if we were OK. They told us it would be best for us to portage the Otter Rapids ahead. I think they felt it was important to tell us that after seeing we had crashed in Little Devil Rapids. We loaded up below the rapids and canoed on to a campsite just above Otter Rapids. We had enough rapids for this day.

It was Saturday night so we toasted with the last of our rum. We hoped for a good wind behind us on Sunday as we had a long way to go to Stanley Mission. Our flight to La Ronge was scheduled for Monday morning from Stanley Mission. All the lakes in this area are long and thin, stretching in a northeast to southwest direction. The glacier carved these out as it went over the shield in that direction.

After breakfast the next morning, we portaged by Otter Rapids. It was well used and in addition to the road and the bridge there was a campground and quite a few people. According to the topographic map the road ended there, but it seemed to go on, probably to some mining camp. We didn't see towns on the road beyond the bridge. Now we were truly in civilization and we also had mosquitoes and blackflies. They seem to like to stay with civilization where they can eat on humans. It also was really the end of super, great fishing, as there were many people fishing in this area.

Wally and I made good time on the first part of Otter Lake to Stony Mountain Portage. Just before the portage we saw an Indian canoe with a sail rig set up. They seemed to be moving along nicely. We got to the Stoney Mountain Portage at the same time they did. It was a couple with three children. The children helped us carry some of the small items across the portage since we gave them some candy. They enjoyed helping us, strange travelers. Then we crossed the small lake and portaged around the falls. Again, we were now near people and lots of black flies and mosquitos.

After the portage the wind was against us and we dodged behind islands as best we could. We rounded a point and could see the flag of Stanley Mission but the wind blew hard down the narrow channel and gigantic waves were crashing at us. We decided to stop and wait for the wind to die down. To pull the canoe to shore, we had to drag the canoe backwards, into the rocky shore. We brought the canoe in but with a lot of grunting and pulling over the rocks with waves splashing in. Now we could take a nap and wait out the wind. We would go on to Stanley Mission when the wind let up.

After we were settled, we saw a huge red canoe with a motor try to land where we had. The waves tossed the canoe against the rocks. With our help, we finally got it up on shore. A couple of ribs of their canoe were cracked on the rocks. The couple in the canoe were Joe and Mary. He was the manager of the Hudson Bay post at Stanley Mission. We made coffee to share with them and we exchanged stories until about 8:30 p.m. when the wind let up. Then we paddled on into Stanley Mission. After we set up our tents we went to Joe and Mary's house for a beer. They were really fun folks and we had an interesting visit.

Then we checked in with the base to let them know we had arrived safely. We learned that, once again, no one knew about us or any flight arrangements. No one would have come looking for us had we not checked in. We had made arrangements with the pilot who flew us into Lac Ile a la Crosse to inform the base at Stanley Mission when we would arrive and that if we didn't, they should look for us. We were pretty disgusted with him until we learned he had been killed in a crash fighting forest fires after he flew us in. It left us with a vague feeling of fear

Wally, Martha, and Rollie ready to fly out

and respect for the Canadian wilderness. It also left us without a flight to La Ronge with most planes busy with fire fighting.

While waiting for word on available flights, we visited the Stanley mission school. It was an eight-room school with four more rooms being added. It looked modern and well-equipped. Across the water is one of the oldest churches in Canada. The Holy Trinity Angelican Church was built between 1854 and 1860. It is the oldest standing building in Saskatchewan. It is a national historic site of Canada. Finally, we arranged a flight in the late afternoon with the mail run in a Beechcraft from La Ronge Airways.

There was a crashed plane in the middle of the river that had caught a pontoon on landing a couple of days before. When our pilot was tying our canoe onto his pontoon he was grumbling about how bad it would be if it came loose. You can't land with a canoe hanging off your pontoon.

On the flight Martha rode in the only available seat, the copilot seat. Wally and I rode in the back. It was a nice flight and we saw all the lakes and forest below with no sign of people. Martha did not like the pilot who once we got in the air reached down and pull up a paperback adult romance book and started to read. She thought he should be paying attention to the flight, not the book with the lewd picture on the front.

Chapter Eleven: Out of the Woods

After landing in La Ronge we found out that they replaced the wrong gasket on the pickup, so we could buy and burn oil again. Then we had a beer and a steak and headed for Flin Flon on 200 miles of gravel road. About 70 miles from Flin Flon we stopped at the Northern Lights Lodge. Their old log cabins were a step up from our tents in the wild. Now we had a toilet, bedding, and breakfast on a table. In the morning after huge breakfast at the lodge we drove on to Flin Flon to see the town with a strange name. Flin Flon was the site of a gold rush in 1910. The mining turned to copper and zinc five years later when a massive copper ore body was found. The story of the name comes from a book Tom Creighton, one of the prospectors that found the ore deposit, picked up along a trail. It's main hero was Josiah Flintbbaty Flonitian, nicknamed Flin Flon. The prospectors named the town after him. A statue of Flin Flon stands in town that was designed by Al Capp, the creator of Lil Abner. We visited the local smelting museum. Then we drove on to The Pas (or Las Pas) and found a garage that could fix the pickup but it needed parts from Swan River. This meant a delay of a couple days before they could fix the truck.

We decided to take the train to Churchill to see where the Churchill River joins Hudson Bay. The Cambrian Hotel was our campsite for the night and we would catch the train to Churchill in the morning. We were entertained by a country band that night after a great meal and a few beers at the hotel. The train in the morning had no lower bunks so we settled for uppers. From the train we saw endless spruce swamps in muskeg, a barren land. The train did go through Thompson where it stopped. The town had grown quite a bit because of mining. Some people got off at Thompson so we were able to book bottom bunks. It was 11:30 p.m. and

Wally, Martha, Sigurd and Rollie

still twilight. The three lower berths made it much easier to get into the bed. The food on the train was delicious and it's easy to like the food after you've been eating in the woods for two weeks. We met a couple from New Mexico, and a chef for construction camps where power lines were being built. The view from the train was the same with spruce, swamps and muskeg. As we traveled the spruce got thinner and we passed a few desolate Indian villages. People told us Thompson had grown from a population of 10 to 30,000 in ten years.

The tour of Churchill was interesting and we enjoyed the museum. We walked down to where the Churchill River flows into Hudson Bay. You can see old Fort Churchill across the water. It is a popular place for watching polar bears and doing research on them. It is also an old sea port from the 1600's. We took the train back to Las Pas and got the pickup. Its gasket was fixed so we didn't need to keep adding oil. We had slept on the train so we dove the pickup straight through to Ely. There we stopped to return the canoe. Cliff Wold was glad we made it and brought back his canoe.

It was an honor to visit with Sigurd Olson in Ely and to give him the report of our trip. He was happy to see us and was interested to find out how the river was and how we did on the trip. Exchanging stories about our trip with this very esteemed author and environmentalist was a thrill. He signed the copy of *The Lonely Land* which we had used as a guide and was covered in stains from the water of the Churchill River. The book was special to him as well, as it was the only one he had seen which was wet by the wind and the waves of the Churchill River. What a great way to finish our trip to the lonely land.

The pickup took us back down interstate highways to Center City. By that time the pickup seemed out of place on highways rather than gravel roads. Martha left the next day for Madison, Wisconsin. She would be leaving her position at the University of Wisconsin in Madison and had accepted a position in the Department of Rehabilitation at the University of Washington in Seattle as a speech pathologist. I became very busy setting up for three weekend Country Music Shows.

Chapter Twelve: What Next?

In the fall Martha was driving to Seattle with her friend Mary. I scheduled to work North and South Dakota so I could meet Martha and Mary in Rapid City for the weekend. We had a great weekend in the Black Hills. They continued on after the weekend to Seattle, stopping at Glacier National Park. While there, Martha visited with my aunt Judith who worked many summers as a park cook. I headed back home by way of music stores in North Dakota. Now I wouldn't be able to visit Martha in Madison anymore.

I contacted the Harptone Guitar Company that I worked for and also Philadelphia Music Company. I knew that neither had a sales representative in Washington or Oregon. So I volunteered to take over those territories. I would be able to visit Martha in Seattle when I made business trips to Washington and Oregon. I was also able to keep my territory in the Midwest. I kept very busy with the new area but about every three months I was able to make trips to Seattle to visit Martha and call on the music stores in the Northwest.

Martha had rented a house on the shore of Lake Sammamish so I had a place to stay when I was in Seattle. One day while calling on a music store in Spokane, I noticed a nearby bookstore. I stopped at the bookstore and noticed a large section of books on the gold rush on the Klondike in the Yukon Territory. It planted a seed about the possibility of a Yukon River trip. When I told Martha she agreed it sounded like another great adventure. Back in Minnesota I called Wally and he was also game.

We began to make plans to canoe the Yukon River from Whitehorse to Dawson City, the route of the gold rushers. There are many books about the gold rush, the Yukon River and Chilkoot Pass. We read quite a few of them. I chose the poetry of the area in *Best Tales of the Yukon* by Robert Service, the novels *Journey* and *Alaska* by James Michener. *Journey* tells the story of gold miners traveling from Edmonton down the Yukon River to Dawson City from the north. Michener wrote about the gold rush which was a big part of the story of *Alaska*, however most of the gold rush actually took place in Canada. He wrote about Skagway and Chilkoot Pass and the Alaskan part of the gold rush, but little about the Canadian section.

Wally found a friend, Kent Stoephen, who was interested in going so we would have four people in two canoes. This would be better than the Churchill trip where we were three in only one canoe. There is safety in numbers. It's better to have a backup canoe and a way for someone to go for help if there is a problem. We thought the Whitehorse to Dawson section where the gold rushers traveled would be the most interesting.

I made a number of trips to Seattle for business which allowed me to visit Martha as well. I spent New Year's there with Martha and some friends. We went skiing at Garibaldi, (now called Whistler Ski Area) near Vancouver. Martha turned out to be a pretty good skier too.

During the winter I started contact people in Whitehorse, Yukon Territory. I talked to John Lammers. He does complete package tours and he understood that we wanted to do the trip on our own, and so he suggested either the Voyager Canoe Club in Whitehorse or the Hudson Bay Company. I decided to contact the Hudson Bay Company because they would do one way canoe trips for us. We had talked about going as far as Circle, Alaska, but that required a customs bond for the canoes. I made arrangements with Hudson Bay Company to provide two canoes for us. We would pick the canoes up in Whitehorse and leave them in Dawson City.

Martha arranged for passage on a cruise ship from Vancouver, B.C. to Skagway, Alaska for her, Wally and I. This is one of the routes people took in gold rush days. But they were not on a Norwegian cruise ship. The three of us would then take the train from Skagway to Whitehorse. Kent Stoephen would meet us in Whitehorse.

From the readings we had done, we learned why so many people made this trip. George Washington Carmack and his two Indian brother-in-laws, Skookum Jim and Tagish Charlie had found gold on Rabbit Creek, a tributary of Thron-duck in the Yukon Territory, Canada, late in the summer of 1896. By the time they got back to Dawson and broke the news it was too late for the news to travel down the Yukon that year. Word of the discovery did not get out until the ship Portland docked in Seattle on July 17, 1897. A reporter then wrote the famous words "a ton of gold" for the world to read. It would trigger the Klondike gold rush which would involve a trip by water and foot of about 1900 miles from Seattle to the Klondike.

We all met in Seattle at the end of June. Wally came in early to visit a friend and some relatives in Seattle. When I arrived in Seattle I did some additional planning for the trip while Martha was still working. The next day I called on a couple of music stores and purchased a metal detector and two gold pans. I thought we could pay for our trip with the gold we panned.

On June 29th, Wally and I met with Martha at her house on Lake Sammamish for a pork chop dinner. We completed planning and packing over the next days. On July 1st I took Martha to work early and went back to her house to do some final packing. Wally and I did a slapstick movie to record our loading of the gear. We picked up Martha from work at the University of Washington hospital and brought her home to get ready to leave. Martha's brother, Chuck, who was a ranger at Mt. Rainier National Park, and his wife, Kathy, drove the three of us to Vancouver where we would catch the ship and begin the adventure.

Chapter Thirteen: The Inside Passage

It was a scenic drive from Seattle to Vancouver but we would see even more wonderful views on the trip. When we arrived at the port in Vancouver we boarded the ship Meteor, a Norwegian cruise ship of the Bremer Line. We said goodbye to Chuck and Kathy and loaded all our gear on board. We settled into our tiny little cabins and enjoyed a delicious meal, the first of many fabulous meals on the cruise ship. We relished these meals as we knew things would change once we were in the wilderness. Today, the first of July, was a little cloudy but it didn't diminish our appreciation of sailing the beautiful inside passage with its thick forests and wilderness waterway.

Since the Churchill River trip Martha and I had become birdwatchers. We enjoyed the variety of gulls and a Bald Eagle sitting on the rocky shore. The Cassin's Auklets were fascinating to watch; we thought the ship would surely run over them but they always scurried out of the way in the nick of time as we approached. We had never before seen a Pigeon Guillemot with its unusual bright orange feet.

We knew our life on board the ship would be in marked contrast to our upcoming camping and canoeing adventure. At dinner we met Elizabeth from England who was the fourth passenger assigned to our table for meals. She was on an around-the-world tour and would be back in London by Christmas. She had spent a year as an English teacher in Belmont, Washington. It was interesting to talk with her and we all shared many stories. After the fabulous dinner, there was a band playing and we joined other guests for dancing. It was fun to dance with Martha; she was good dancer and we had not danced before. We all enjoyed the cruise and especially

Mendenhall Glacier

Wally; being a tight Swede he liked the martinis for only $0.60 since there was no tax on the open water.

At Ketchikan the ship stopped for a short time. We took a cab to the Totem Park where there's a large collection of totem poles. Wally and I made another slapstick movie throwing a can back and forth to illustrate the Ketchikan Can Dance. Martha was embarrassed but under pressure she did run the camera for us so we could make the movie.

At a stop in Juneau we took a tour of the Mendenhall Glacier where we saw many Arctic Terns. We told no tern jokes this time. After a dinner on shore we toured a gold mine and saw a local gay nineties type show in the theater that was located down in the mine. Then we went back to the ship for the Fourth of July celebration: dancing and a great party. We knew we would be sorry to wrap up this section of our trip and transition to the wilderness.

Chapter Fourteen: Getting to Whitehorse

On July 5th we arrived in Skagway at about 8:00 a.m. We had to get up early after the celebration of the 4th of July. We unloaded our gear and checked into the Sourdough Motel.

The Indian name Skagway means Home of the North Wind. It became the gateway to the Klondike where gold rushers would choose to go up White Pass or Chilkoot Pass. White Pass was known for the use of pack horses. It was a sea of mud and many horses died there. Chilkoot Pass was a hard climb by foot up a steep slope of ice and snow. Years later a railroad was built up White Pass. It was a tough engineering feat. At the time of the gold rush Skagway became Alaska's largest city. There were about 80 saloons and it was rumored that at least one corpse turned up every morning. The Skagway crime boss was Soapy Smith. Legend has it that Soapy Smith's gang stole about thirty percent of the supplies miners brought to Skagway. Soapy killed and was killed by Frank Reid in the same gunfight. We took a walk to see their graves in the old cemetery.

After unloading our gear at the motel we ate lunch then walked up Diversity Mountain to Diversity Lake. Along the way we saw a Varied Thrush. A Golden Eagle and a Common Raven seen high along the trail seemed to be attacking each other. Once down from the mountain we said goodbye to Elizabeth as she boarded the cruise ship to continue on through the inside passage. We enjoyed a delicious fresh caught salmon dinner before going back to the motel.

On July 6th we boarded the White Pass train at 10:30 in the morning on the way to Whitehorse. It was a beautiful and exciting trip up the White Pass. We could see remains of the old trail where many miners had tried to cross and lost their horses. Many horse bones still can be seen on the trail. Due to the quagmire of mud on the trail in 1897, it is said 3000 horses died on the trail. Jack London wrote "The horses died like mosquitoes in the first frost". Most gold rushers chose the Chilkoot Pass instead. Later we would walk across Chilkoot Pass from east to west instead of west to east as the gold rushers did. It did not have the mud but steep rocky slopes instead.

The train stopped at Lake Bennett where everyone got off and had a family-style lunch. When the gold rushers made it over Chilkoot Pass they had to build boats and cross Lake Lindeman and Lake Bennett. Between Lake Bennet and the Yukon at Whitehorse there was a rough canyon and a bad set of rapids. Now there is a power dam with a reservoir. The train continued on to Whitehorse after lunch. When we got off the train at Whitehorse we found Kent Stoephen waiting for us. He had hitchhiked, on his own, from Minneapolis. At the Hudson Bay post we learned that our canoes were expected in Whitehorse on Wednesday evening. After dinner in town we set up camp a couple miles north of town at the Robert Service Campground on the banks of the Yukon River.

The next morning it was raining lightly when we got up and walked to the Hudson Bay Company in town to check again on our canoes. After a nice lunch at the Whitehorse Inn we walked to see two old excursion boats, the Casa and the Whitehorse. They were in sad shape and had not been in the water for years. We bought some groceries and walked back to the campsite to make supper.

It was still raining lightly the next morning. The campsite was a quiet, pleasant place with many trees and many birds including White Crown Sparrows, Mountain Bluebirds, Bank

Swallows, Juncos, Grey Jays, and Cliff Swallows. We were still new at birding and added many birds to our growing lists.

We checked again on the canoes, and they said they would be there that night so we could leave Thursday morning. We took time to explore Whitehorse, visiting the museum in the Whitehorse Library and Sam McGee's cabin. At the government office we got maps, fishing licenses, and a fire permit. There we met Lynne Taylor who knew and was a friend of Sigurd Olson. We enjoyed talking canoe adventures and Sigurd's appreciation of the northern wilderness with him. It was still raining when we called the Hudson Bay Company and asked them to bring the canoes to our campsite on the river just below the Whitehorse Dam, south of town.

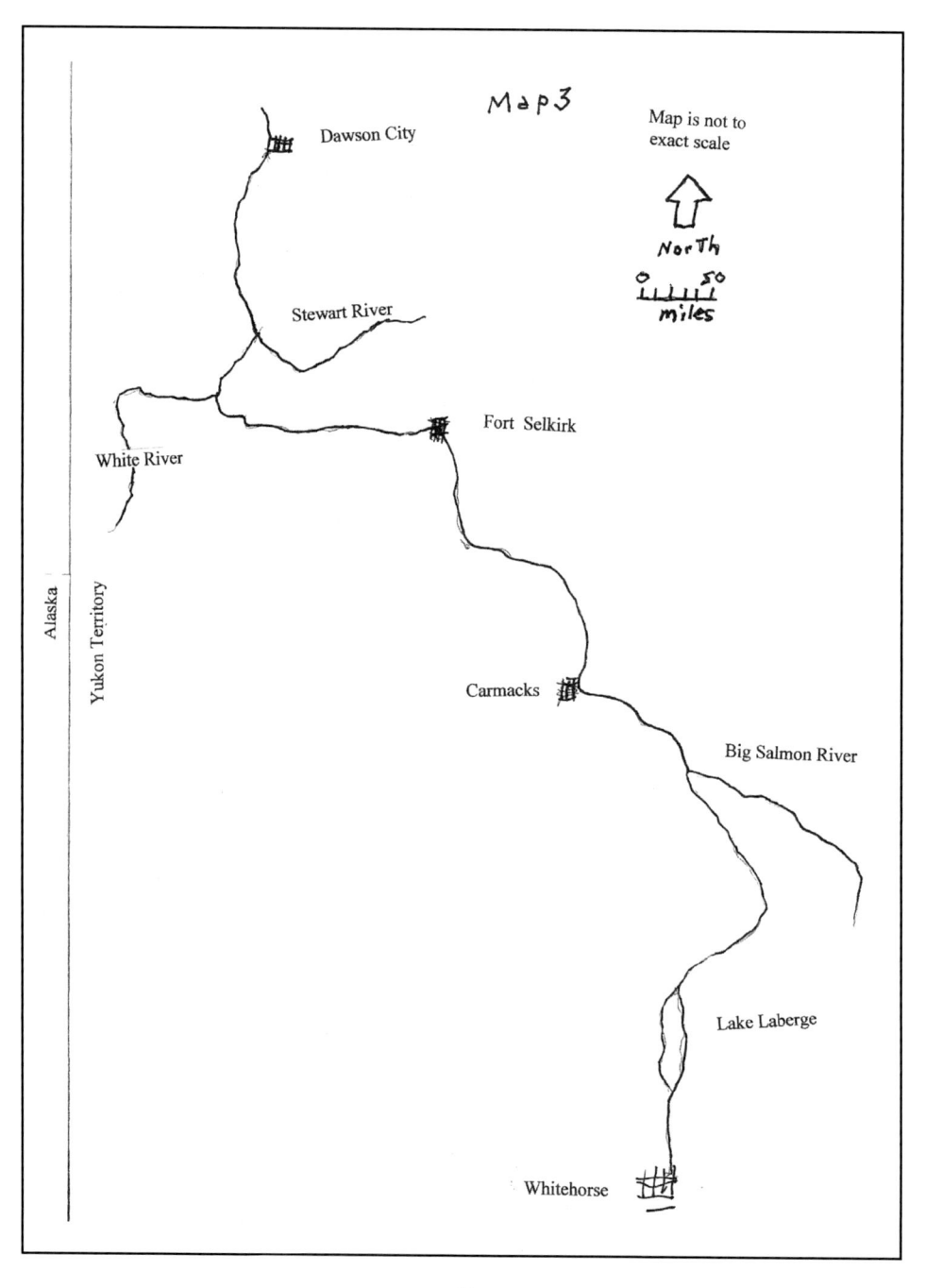

Chapter Fifteen: On the Water Again

On July 9th we woke early and were eating breakfast when the canoes arrived. It was sunny and the rain had stopped. A great day to get on the river. We loaded the canoes with our gear and also the suitcases that we would drop off in Whitehorse at the Hudson Bay post to be held until our return. Wally and I made some last minute purchases and Martha and Kent sent postcards. At 2:15 p.m. we were off, in our canoes and on our way, at last. The real adventure was beginning. (See Map 3)

The current was fast so we made 25 miles into Lake Laberge by 9:30 p.m. We had crossed a shallow and windy area. The daylight lasts long up here in the north. It was still light when we got to bed about midnight. A light rain started and put us to sleep. During the day we had seen a group of 14 Loons, another Golden Eagle, and many terns, gulls, and ducks. The Harlequin Duck was our unforgettable favorite as it swam just ahead of us in the river for quite a distance.

Our campsite was on the west side of the lake so we had been out of the wind. On July 10th, Friday, we were up at 8:30 a.m. and on the water by 12:00 noon. The sun was shining and we had a strong wind pushing us down the lake. It was fun riding the swells as we made good time flying down the lake.

Many years later, in the summer of 2003, Martha and I and a group of friends did a kayak trip on the west coast of Sweden. One day the guide asked if anyone wanted to go out into the North Sea as we were sheltered by islands. A few of us did and once out from behind the island we found huge swells a little like Lake Laberge but maybe three times bigger. After a quarter of a mile we came back to the shelter of the islands.

Canoes on the shore of Lake Laberge

When we got hungry we brought the canoes together for lunch of hard tack (a dry, hard type of bread), peanut butter, bacon chips, and cherry drink. It was clear that if we ate like that we won't lose any weight. We paddled by a batch of baby gulls, more loons, and White-winged Scoters. That afternoon the wind came up so strong we made camp early, about 6:00 p.m. It was a great campsite and after a freeze-dried turkey supreme supper we tried fishing, but no luck.

On Saturday we decided to start early so we could get up the lake before the wind picked up. Wally was to get us up at 4:00 a.m. but he was still sleepy so he woke us at 5:15 a.m. After Red River cereal and peaches we were on the lake cruising by 8:30 a.m. Again, we enjoyed the big swells that pushed us along. Soon the wind picked up and we had to pull into a cove for shelter. Once on shore we looked out on the lake and realized we got into this cove just in time. The lake gets rough for canoes real fast. While we waited out the wind we found an old trapper cabin. It was interesting but littered with junk. The sun was warm and we laid out our sleeping bags to sunbathe. I think Robert Service would turn over in his grave or write a new poem if he saw someone sunbathing on the shore of Lake Laberge. What would Sam Magee think? Martha, Kent and I took a swim in the lake and found that it's cold; we were in for a second and back out quickly. Later we read and Kent walked up the nearby ridge for a view. It was relaxing to enjoy this wild spot without a concern about meeting a schedule.

After lunch the wind let up so we headed out again. By 6:00 p.m. we were only five miles from the end of Lake Laberge, but again the wind forced us to shore for shelter. We cooked supper and started out again at 8:00 p.m. The wind had calmed some but it seemed risky as we paddled across the upper end of the lake. It was a wild ride but we got onto the river, out of the wind and made camp.

Since we had eaten supper at the last break, all we had to do was set up our tents and have a hot rum drink and go to bed. Near our campsite was a wreck of an old river boat partly buried in the sand.

The wreck was called the Casa and it made us think of the Robert Service poem about the cremation of Sam McGee. We could not tell if it had a boiler where a fire could be started and do a cremation. We were relieved to have made it across Lake Laberge so easily and only had to stop three times to get out of the wind. In James Michener's book "Alaska" he follows the route of the gold rush to Dawson City but does not mention Lake Laberge. This seems surprising because Lake Laberge was an unforgettable part of the trip for us. Mitchner mentions that Robert Service in his poem, "The Cremation of Sam McGee" spells Lake Laberge as Lake Lebarge so that it fit in the poem better.

In the morning we looked back at Lake Laberge and you could see the big rollers crashing in. It made us really glad we had crossed to the river the night before. Wally got up and was taking down his tent while I started the fire for breakfast. We investigated the hulk of the Casa and took some pictures. It was a sunny day, but a little cool. The scenery was fantastic along the river which was quite narrow now with a variety of birds. Harlequin Ducks were swimming ahead of us and the Violet-green Swallows flew overhead. We saw Yellow Warblers and some Belted Kingfishers.

Wally and Kent stopped at a small stream to see if they could catch some fish. They didn't have any luck and they had to paddle hard to catch up with Martha and me. We hadn't seen others on the river but came upon some people that morning: a group of firefighters and later a family of five from California in their Klepper Fold Boats. We made camp by a small stream. After a try at fishing we were tired from 57 miles of paddling and went, not to bed, but to tent.

Rollie standing on the wreck of the Casa

In the morning Wally, the Bourgeois, slept in until 9:00 a.m. and he woke up to see me land a grayling. With that I won a six pack of beer from Wally and I again was a master angler. I caught another grayling and filleted them both. We had them for dessert, after a breakfast of oatmeal and bacon. We broke camp about 1:00 p.m. and paddled to where the Big Salmon River joins the Yukon. The Big Salmon had a lot of glacier water, white and creamy, a change from the water in the Yukon which was mostly clear. We fished for an hour and a half but had no luck.

While we were fishing, Martha was reading the book *Open Horizons* by Sigurd Olson. When we left to go on to the camp where the Welch River joins the Yukon she discovered she had left her book by the Big Salmon River. Once we set up camp at the Welch River we tried to walk back along the shore to get the book. The river current was too fast to paddle up river, so we decided to walk. We did not go far through the thick brush before we decided it couldn't be done.

After the trip Wally called Sigurd Olson and told him about Martha leaving the book on the shore of the Yukon River. Olson replaced the book for Martha and inscribed in it to her with a warning "next time don't leave the book in such an inaccessible place" sincerely Sig. The book is still on the sandbar where the Big Salmon River runs into the Yukon. Maybe someone will stop and pick it up someday.

The family that was traveling in the Fold Boats stopped to visit as they went past. After supper we tried fishing but no luck. Fishing on the Yukon is a far different experience than fishing on the Churchill. The next morning we woke at 8:00 a.m. After breakfast we climbed the ridge behind our campsite. What a spectacular view. Then we ran down towards the campsite in the ankle deep sphagnum moss. It was so soft that running down through it felt a little

Indian grave houses checked out by Wally, Rollie and Kent

like skiing powder snow. We rebounded back and forth and leaped up and down on our descent. A fall in it would be like a fall in soft feathers. We climbed up and bounced down a couple more times. Later we thought it could be bad if we twisted an ankle or broke a bone with such wild activity and no ski patrol here in the wilderness to rescue us.

At 11:45 a.m. we were on the way to Clear Creek where we had lunch. We passed the Nickerson family in their fold boats as they floated having lunch. Today it rained off and on but when you are prepared a little rain is no problem. We passed an old dredge that had been used for gold mining. That night we camped by an old Indian cemetery where little cabins had been built over each grave. We looked inside the windows of the little cabins and there were chairs and tables with dishes set up so that the spirits could live in the cabin.

We got to sleep about 11:15 p.m. after another fun day. Tomorrow we would get to Carmacks, the first settlement since we left Whitehorse.

We woke up at 6:00 a.m. to a beautiful sunny day. The temperature was about 35 degrees and there was frost on the grass. Our new a system of getting started had us on the river by 8:00 a.m. The current was fast and the wind was behind us so we landed at Carmacks by 11:30 a.m. We reported to the Royal Canadian Mounted Police Station and bought some flies that were guaranteed to catch grayling. After a couple of beers in the local tavern we headed on down the river. Not much to see in town so we paddled on for a total of 57 miles for the day.

Wally and I tried fishing with our new flies but no luck. It's a good thing we had food with us and didn't depend on catching our food. At the campsite that night there were some nice pot holes in the rocks that had water in them, and the water was nice and warm from the sun. So we washed clothes and had warm baths and went to bed at 9:30 p.m. We all agreed Martha's cooking was great. The Bourgeois got us up at 6:00 a.m. again. We were soon up and moving with the temperature at a cold 37 degrees, but the sun was shining. After Red River cereal, bacon and canned pears we left at 8:15 a.m. and sped along in the fast current with wind on our backs most of the time. Aspen, willow, and alders grow along the shore and up on top of the hills are spruce. We noticed Indian fishnets along the river in preparation for the coming salmon run. Light rain started about 10:00 a.m.

As we floated in the current Martha tried fishing and caught two grayling on flies. Wally and I threw in our lines and got a couple more. We had grayling for dessert after supper that night. They were small but tasty. After we got our tents up we noticed huge bear tracks on the shore. Martha's footprint would fit entirely within the track.

It was scary to camp there, but we had been told that the bears in this area are hunted and so they stay away from people. We hope they were right about that. We made another foolish slapstick movie about Martha scaring away a bear. We later learned that many people carry bear spray in this area and also on Chilkoot Pass.

The two rapids we had that day were not tough. We enjoyed Five Fingers Rapids, it was fast water but no rocks in our way. We got too far to the right, on Rink Rapids, to get into the main part where the white horses were. After 45 miles that day we got to bed about 9:15 p.m.

We woke about 6:15 a.m. and had breakfast of pancakes and the bacon we bought in Carmacks. We left camp at 8:15 a.m. on the warmest day so far. On the river there was no wind and the consistent Yukon current moved us along nicely.

Fresh big bear tracks

Wally and Danny looking over the moose meat

Fort Selkirk was our stop at noon where we met Danny Roberts and his family. They are a native family who live there as caretakers. The day before Danny had shot a two year old bull moose and they were busy quartering and butchering it.

They cut the meat into strips and smoke it and dry it. It's like moose jerky when it's done. Martha was curious about it and Danny's wife took her into the shed and cut off a piece of the dried meat that was done. We had seen many flies on the meat but when she gave it to Martha to taste, Martha felt she could not refuse to eat it. Martha kept it in her mouth until she had a chance, away from the family, to spit it out.

Danny's son

Fort Selkirk Church

    Danny's family also sets nets for salmon. They have nine dogs to pull the dogsleds in the winter for the trap line and to go to the nearest store. I think he gets paid a guaranteed amount for guarding the buildings of the old fort. Many of the buildings were in good shape. The schoolhouse had desks and a blackboard. It looked like you could start class there the next day. The little church even had stained glass windows. It was fascinating to learn about the history and about Danny's life in Fort Selkirk on the Yukon. There are no other inhabitants in the area; only Danny and his family live here now.

    We left Fort Selkirk at 1:30 p.m. and floated together as we ate lunch. The rocky island we found for the night had a nice spot for our tents in the open and away from mosquitoes. Martha made a great bannock to have with the chicken romanoff supper. After a 60 mile day, we were in bed by 8:30 p.m. Each day we found we got up earlier and stopped earlier. Initially, the length of daylight hours probably kept us paddling longer.

    On Saturday, we were on the river after a breakfast of oatmeal and peach sauce. A sunny day and we were moving at eight to ten miles per hour if we did a little paddling. The river began to get wider and slower and the wind came towards us. With the canoes held together for lunch we saw a big bull moose come out of the woods on the left shore. A little farther on a black bear was on the right shore. We paddled over towards the bear to get a picture. He didn't run off but got into the water and started to swim toward us. Martha thought that we got a little too close to get movies. He seemed to be very curious and had no fear of us at all.

    At Kirkman Creek we made camp. There were remains of an old post office but that was all that was left of the town. I tried panning in the creek but found no gold. I also got out the metal detector but all I found were cans and junk. This campsite had a full complement of mosquitoes

Wally, Kent and Rollie setting up a sail

and blackflies. We missed the frequent walleye fillets we had on the Churchill, but Martha made another good bannock to go with supper.

Sunday, July 19th was a beautiful day with fog on the river which soon burned off. After eggs and bacon crisps we were on the river by 8:15 a.m. About 11:00 a.m. we saw a cow moose and her calf. We floated quietly and were able to approach close enough for a good view. Martha got some pictures with her camera but for some reason my eight millimeter movie camera wouldn't run until they had walked back into the woods. We hadn't seen anyone for several days but we stopped at Stewart Creek where we met the Bjorions. They live there year round and do freighting on the river in the summer. Their children go to school by correspondence. Both of the adults run trap lines with their dog teams in the winter. We had planned to stay at Sixty Miles Creek, but when we arrived there was a group of Indians setting up for the salmon run. We went on and a couple of miles downstream we found an open site where we set up camp and stayed away from the mosquitoes. After 55 miles and another supper we went to sleep, but heard the wind blow all night.

After breakfast Wally thought that with the wind we should set up a sail with the two canoes tied together. We cut poles and tied two of them upright to hold the tarp. It looked like it would work great and it did until the wind changed to the north which was against us. We took down the tarp but left the canoes tied together. The sun was out and we hardly paddled as the current moved us along at about 10 miles per hour.

At Garner Creek we pulled to shore to walk along the creek for about a couple of miles. It was an old trail and gave us a chance to stretch our legs. The walk was through wild Yukon country. We saw new birds and many that we could not identify because they moved too fast and stayed in the thicket. That night we had steak that we had purchased at Stewart Creek.

There was a Golden Eagle soaring over us and we heard cries from baby eagles. With binoculars we could see the nest on the high cliff across from our camp. One eaglet was on the nest and the other was out of the nest on the ledge.

The next day we planned to arrived in Dawson. Another nice breakfast in the morning from Martha's kitchen and we were on the water by 8:00 a.m. In the morning we said goodbye to one of the eaglets while the others were hiding. We arrived in Dawson about 10:30 a.m. While the others stayed by the canoes and our gear, I went looking for a place to set up our tents. I got the OK to set up in the yard of the Northern Star Motel. The canoes were left by the river and we carried our gear to the motel area, set up our tents and had lunch in town.

Chapter Sixteen: Dawson City

After a sit-down lunch, at a table inside, we went back for hot showers and a change of clothes. The laundromat was our next stop where we washed clothes. That night we had a fresh salmon dinner and went to the Dawson City Gaslight Follies at the Palace Grand Theatre. The show was based on Robert Service tales including, *The Shooting of Dan McGrew* and *The Cremation of Sam McGee*. Much of it set to music. It was the perfect show for us; it was well done and we loved it.

In the afternoon we had met the man from the trucking company who would take our canoes back to Whitehorse. Wally, Martha and I decided to take the bus back to Whitehorse, then the train to Lake Bennett and hike over Chilkoot Pass. We felt by hiking Chilkoot Pass we would get a broader perspective of the Gold Rush days. It would be a tough walk because we didn't have backpacks and would have to carry our gear in our Duluth Packs.

Wednesday July 22nd we walked up the Klondike River for a tour of the goldfields. One claim there is owned by the city of Dawson for tourists to try their hand at panning gold. We had carried our gold pans a long way and were eager to use them.

We found a few flecks of gold and it was interesting to see how panning for gold is done. It was fun to see how the little flakes of gold would show up in the black sand in the pan as you swished it back and forth. After about three hours on claim number six at the fork of Rabbit Creek (now called the Bonanza) and the Thron-duck (now called the Eldorado) we got some gold color and a little for souvenirs. Unfortunately it was not enough to cover our gold rush adventure.

Martha and Wally digging dirt to be panned

Rollie, Kent and Wally panning for gold

    Back in town we walked around to see the Robert Service cabin and the Jack London cabin, which had been moved into town. We met a couple from Louisiana, he played piano after supper at the Flora Dora Restaurant. They told us the White Pass Railroad was on strike and not running. That could disrupt our plan to get from Whitehorse to Chilkoot Pass. We decided to check at the airport and see if we could get a bush pilot to fly us into Lake Lindeman. From Lake Lindeman, where the town used to be, we could start up Chilkoot Pass. It was now two weeks since we had left Whitehorse.

    We explored Dawson learning more about its history and the gold rush era. We joined a tour to the ship graveyard crossing the Yukon on a ferry. It had a number of old ships that traveled the Yukon years ago. After returning from the ship graveyard, we had a couple of beers at the Sourdough Saloon. We toured the Gold Room in the bank where the gold was melted down into gold bars. At 4:00 p.m. we went to the Robert Service cabin where Graham Campbell, an actor from the Gaslight Follies sat on the porch in a rocking chair dressed as Robert Service and read Robert Service poetry. Again we heard "The Shooting of Dan McGrew" and "The Cremation of Sam McGee."

    I took my pad and did a few sketches of some of the old buildings in Dawson.

Old Post Office

St Andrews Church

Meeker's Place   70

Red Feather Saloon   70

At 6:30 p.m. we saw an Indian walk into the back of a restaurant with a huge fresh salmon across his back. We went into the restaurant and asked for salmon steak from the salmon that was just been brought in. It was an absolutely delicious meal. We're not sure it was from the same salmon the Indian had brought in, but we like to think so.

On Friday we got up early and hiked up the mountain on the back side of Dawson. We made it to the top in a little over two hours and the view was fantastic. Wally walked back down while Martha and I stayed up on the ridge where we were entertained by several Common Ravens. They would fly over and take turns showing off. One would fly low and then flip upside down as he glided by us. Another one would fly by and hang one leg down. They continued the show for us for a long while before leaving. We have read several accounts since of Ravens playing on the air currents, we are sure these were not only playing, but showing off their skills for us as well. It was an unforgettable performance in an unforgettable place overlooking Dawson and the Yukon.

That evening we separated our gear for the Chilkoot Pass. We would send home items we didn't need and didn't want to carry over the pass.

We all had showers and got to bed by 11:30 p.m. although it was still light. Wally read in the Whitehorse paper that a 22 year old had drowned when his canoe tipped in the Yukon that week, he was not wearing a life vest. A grim reminder of the strength and treachery the wild rivers of the north may deal out to those who do not respect them.

Saturday morning we got up at 5:15 a.m. so we would be ready to take the 7:30 a.m. bus back to Whitehorse. Kent helped us carry our gear to the bus depot. Kent was traveling on into Alaska but not by canoe. We said our goodbyes and boarded the bus for a 330 mile ride to Whitehorse. It was an interesting ride. We didn't have to paddle, but just watch the scenery go by. At Whitehorse we shipped gear home that we didn't need and had left at the Hudson Bay Co. At the airport we made arrangements for a flight to Lake Lindeman at 10:00 a.m. the next day.

We set up camp at the Robert Service Campground again and walked to town for supper so we wouldn't have to cook. After supper Martha sorted out the provisions while Wally and I enjoyed a beer. Martha and I kept a tent and Wally kept a tarp to sleep under. On the bus from Dawson we met two boys who had tipped in the Five Fingers Rapids on the Yukon. Their canoe had floated about a quarter of a mile down stream; they had to swim to the sandbar where it stopped. They said the water was very cold and they suffered a lot. By the time they got to their canoe and got things together they had lost car keys and other valuables. We felt lucky to have survived the journey so far.

Chapter Seventeen: Chilkoot Pass

Wally was up at 7:30 a.m. and after a shower woke Martha and me. We ate cold cereal, shouldered our packs and hiked the mile and a half to the seaplane base. Our total weight was 600 pounds for the three of us and our gear. The pilot said "I hope we can get this plane off the water with that kind of weight". Martha and I sat in the back seats, each with a Duluth Pack in our laps. Then the pilot said he hoped he didn't hit any the floating logs that are in the water. Martha, who has a fear of flying, was not at all happy with the situation. We all felt safer when we were in the air and none of the pilot's fears had materialized. Before long we landed safely on the south end of Lake Lindeman. There was no dock so we had to jump into a couple feet of water and wade to shore.

We set up our boots to dry while we had some lunch. Many of the gold rushers came to Lake Lindeman from the pass to build boats and start the long trip to Dawson.

At 12:30 p.m. we started up the trail. It started raining about 3:30 p.m. so we set up camp after we had gone about three miles through an absolutely beautiful landscape. It's amazing how beautiful this pass is, but it's a tough one if you're carrying all your gear and you're going to go looking for gold, we were doing it for fun. The rain gave us a chance to take a nap until about 6:00 p.m. As we were preparing supper, two couples who had just come over the pass came by and set up camp near us. After supper we visited with them and heard about their experiences on the Chilkoot Pass. (See Map 4)

Wally landing on the south shore of Lake Lindeman

Map 4

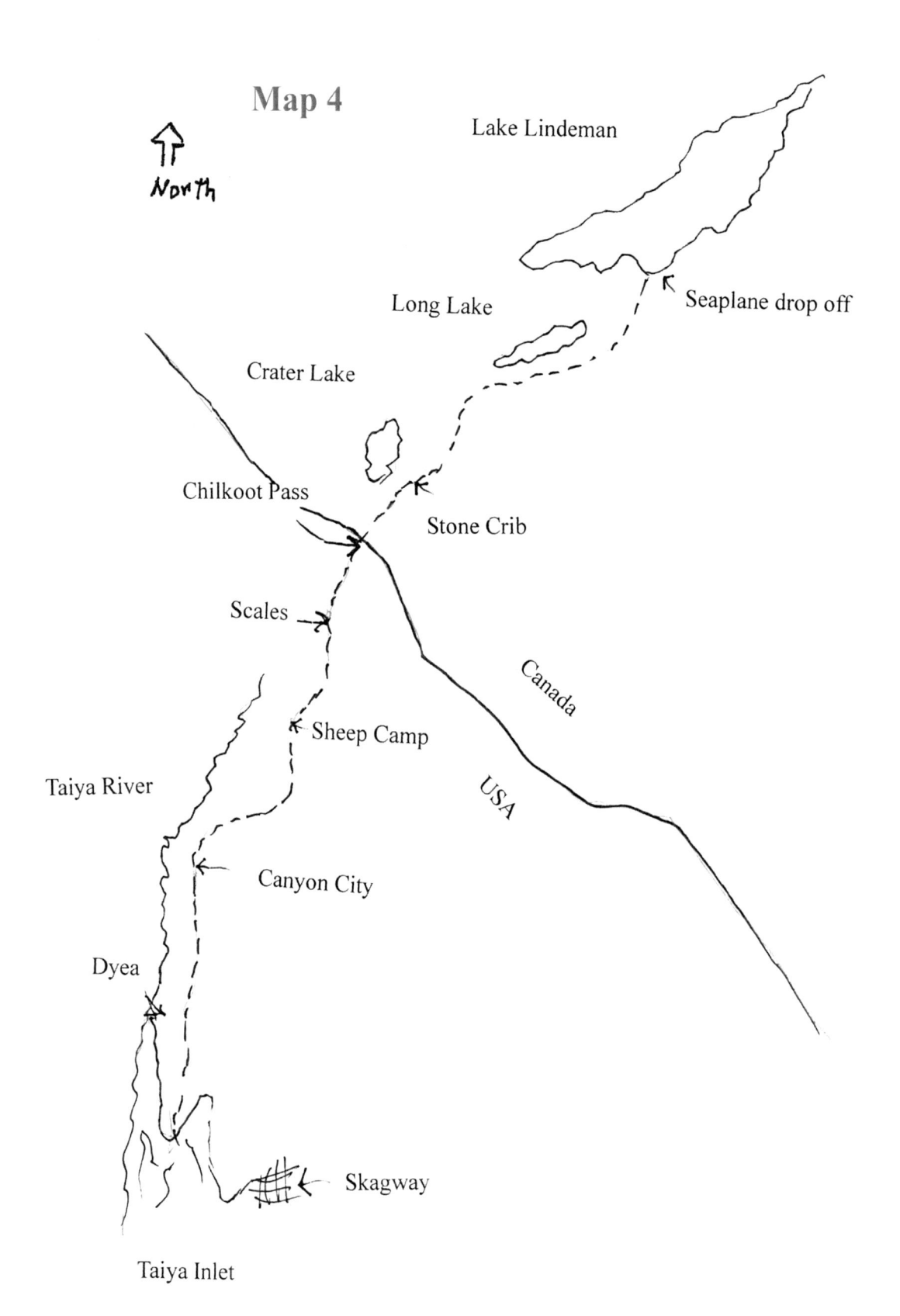

↑ North

Lake Lindeman

Seaplane drop off

Long Lake

Crater Lake

Chilkoot Pass

Stone Crib

Scales

Canada

USA

Sheep Camp

Taiya River

Canyon City

Dyea

Skagway

Taiya Inlet

In the morning we got up at 6:00 a.m. and had breakfast. We stayed and talked to Bob Stevens and Maude, the couple from California. It is always of interest to talk with other people who love to spend time in the wilderness and hear what they have done and why. The trail was beautiful with little lakes and spruce trees. There was some snow on the ground and a blue sky above. While following a small stream we saw our first Rock Ptarmigan. As the scenery got better Wally thought it looked like the Alps. He thought that Martha looked like Heidi and he was the old man in the movie.

The next camp was at Crater Lake. Now we were above treeline so we had trouble finding firewood. We searched for roots and driftwood and whatever we could find to make a cooking fire. We were tired from the hike and we had no way to stake down the tent so we used rocks. I found a flat place. It was covered with snow, but I tried it anyway. Wally founded a dry spot for his tarp to sleep under. Wally also sat on a rock with bare feet in the sun because his feet were killing him from the boots and hiking. He said the sun made his feet feel relaxed so he could handle another day. We were tired, so we had a double ration of Canadian Windsor as we had none that morning. Martha noticed that the floor of the tent was wet so we decide to move our tent off the snow to dry ground even though it was not level. We saw our first Bohemian Waxwings, they are like large Cedar Waxwings. They are a beautiful and unique bird; we knew right away what it was, although none of us had seen one before.

We had done five miles with Duluth Packs. Duluth Packs are large canvas carrying bags with straps made especially for canoeing. They are perfect for canoeing and fit very nicely into the canoe. They work fine for portages but for long all day hikes they are difficult. For the long hike we tried using duct tape to connect the straps of the Duluth Pack to the back of our belts. This way the pack rides higher on your back. It still was not like real backpacks but it sure helped. We were lucky to have sunny days so far. Chilkoot Pass is known for being foggy with drizzling rain most of the time. After hunting around we found enough wood to make a fire for breakfast.

We left Crater Lake about 9:00 a.m. and reached the top of the pass about 11:30 a.m. This last part up the pass we were walking on snow, but we had no slips or slides. It had been a good idea to get walking sticks back where there was wood. It would have been hard without a walking stick. Now we would have to climb down the steep west slope.

The view from the top of the pass was spectacular. We were exceptionally fortunate that it was clear and sunny offering clear views down into the valley on the west side all the way to Taiya Inlet. On the vast majority of days there is no view at all, other than the fog and clouds. One account of going over the pass said the fog was so thick you could hardly see your feet. We looked around for artifacts as this spot was full of gold miner's history. Mostly we found a lot of debris of little interest. We looked at the rock crib which had been the top terminal for the cable lift which carried supplies up the pass. I tried my metal detector which I had carried a long way but found nothing of interest. The pass is the border between Canada and the U.S. In gold rush days, miners crossing over the pass were required to have gear for a year, all of which had to be hauled up the steep west side of the pass. Over 20,000 gold miners crossed the pass on their way to the gold fields. Very few found gold. We crossed over going east to west going home with our little flecks of gold from the Klondike.

From the top we found it difficult to climb down. We had thought we would have it easy going down, not having to climb up the steep side.

The first part drops down 800 feet in only half a mile and had large boulders to climb over. It was very steep. With the Duluth Packs on our backs we found it best to go backwards much

Martha and Wally cooking by the river

Rollie setting up the tent on snow

Wally and Rollie walking on the snow in this wild land

of the time. We almost felt we should use a rope on the steepest down slopes but we were on a canoe trip and not a climbing trip.. no ropes. Slowly we worked our way down. When it flattened out at what was called the scales we stopped for lunch. At the bottom of the steep section of the trail we looked up and wondered how we had made it down. After lunch we hiked on to the Sheep Camp Shelter which was about three and a half miles down the valley and dropped 2,800 feet. We met two boys coming up the trail. We met only the two boys and the two couples from California on the entire pass. This was 1970, and now if you plan to cross the pass you need a permit and only 50 people are allowed on the trail per day. About 4,000 people hike it each year. A big change. The sun was hot and the scenery interesting. There were no mosquitoes.

    At Sheep Camp there was a log shelter with eight bunks. A family of eight had taken all of the bunks so Wally set up on the floor. I put up the tent for Martha and me. The shelter was meant for overnight stays for people traveling over the pass; not for extended stays. Wally was not pleased when he found out the family had been there for a week and planned to stay longer. When Wally woke at 5:30 a.m. he tried to dress and roll up his mat and sleeping bag without waking the family. At the height of the gold rush Sheep Camp had 16 hotels, 14 restaurants and 3 saloons.

    We ate breakfast and headed out at 9:00 a.m. The trail to Canyon City Ruins was easy hiking. At Canyon City we found a huge boiler made in 1886 which was used as a steam powered electric power plant, as well as many old buildings. Martha made bannock with leftover pancake mix which we would enjoy with bacon the next morning. Martha and I set up the tent and Wally found a little cabin he could sleep in. Wally woke up several times during the night in the cabin from the wind banging a door of a nearby building. Martha and I didn't hear it. Wally found he had invaded the home of small rodents that made a "chit chit" noise most of the night.

Going up the pass

Wally called Martha and me about 5:00 a.m. and went down to the stream to clean up. When he returned I had a fire started and Martha had the coffee on. We enjoyed our last adventure breakfast of bannock and bacon. It would be the last one Martha would have to cook for a while. At 7:00 a.m. we left camp and took the trail to a cable lift over the Tawai River. We were disappointed to see the rope to pull the car back to our side had been broken by a fallen tree. We had to retrace our way a mile back to the other trail. When we got to the other trail I headed on ahead to get to the road and hitchhike into town to get a taxi to come back for Martha and Wally and the gear. It was about a mile and a half of rugged terrain to the main road. If the rope had not been broken we would have crossed the river and had a better trail. When I got to the road I started walking towards town. I didn't catch a ride. When Wally and Martha got to the main road at the Iron Bridge a man with a camper said he would take them to Skagway for $10. That sounded like a great deal and they picked me up on the road along the way.

At Skagway we talked to a pilot at the hardware store who would fly us to Juneau for $75. At the Juneau Airport we discovered that all the flights to Seattle were filled. Our luck with flights continued to be consistently bad. We went into the restaurant and had a fine meal. It was a little unusual for us to eat while sitting in a chair at a table. Word came of some cancellations, our luck with flights had improved. We would get on the flight to Seattle at 5:00 p.m. and land in Seattle at 7:00 p.m.

Wally's relatives met him, and Martha's brother and wife met Martha and me at the airport. Wally traveled back to Minnesota with his friend Harold. I stayed for a couple days and then headed back to Minnesota.

Wally climbing down the west side of Chilkoot Pass.

At the end of Robert Service's poem L'Envoi [1907] he wrote:

You may recall that sweep of savage splendor,
    That land that measures each man at his worth,
And feel in memory, half fierce, half tender,
    The brotherhood of men that know the North.

I returned to Seattle again to see Martha and we were married in July of 1971. The greatest adventures are what lie ahead.

Martha and Wally - watch your step on this area

Glossary

Bannock. The original camping bread attributed to native North American tribes, made in a frying pan.

Bourgeois. The leader of a voyageur band.

Bow. Front of the canoe.

Customs Bond. A bond to guarantee that a canoe taken into the U.S. is returned to Canada.

Daredevil. A red and white spoon type of bait with a treble hook on the end.

Duffer. The person sitting in the middle of the canoe and not paddling.

Duluth Pack. A large canvas bag with straps for hauling gear in a canoe, named for Duluth Minnesota.

Factor. The manager of a Hudson Bay Post and Store.

Grayling. A trout-like fish with a fin on it's back.

Hardtack. A hard, thin bread that keeps well on trips without refrigeration.

Hay Stacks. Waves in the rapids with round tops.

Ice Roads. Roads cleared over the ice by plows to enable vehicles to drive to villages in the north during the winter.

Lift Over. A very short portage on the side of a rapids or falls where you can lift the canoe over without unloading it.

Line The Canoe. Guide the canoe along the side of the rapids with lines or ropes attached to the front and back.

Portage. A trail or path on which to carry your canoe and gear around a rapids or falls.

Rapala. A plug type of bait invented in Finland.

Rollers. Round waves out in a lake or a large body of water created by wind.

Shield Country. The area of North America scraped down to hard rock by the continental glacier.

Spouts. Water in the rapids that seems to jump up.

Stern. Back of the canoe.

Strip Canoe. A canoe made of narrow strips of wood.

Wild Horses. Big waves in the rapids that drop into your canoe. In John Wesley Powell's The Exploration of the Colorado River and it's Canyons. In about 1869 Powell mentions a conversation with an Indian named Pariats who told him about one of the members of his tribe in the rapids in a canyon. The Indian said "The rocks h-e-a-p , h-e-a-p high; the water go h-oo-woogh, hoo-woogh; water-pony heap buck;water catch em; no see um indian any more. Maybe since 1869 ponyes in rapids have become horses.

Yacht Mop. A small mop without handles to dry the bottom of the canoe.

About the Author

Roland Westman, known as Rollie, was born in Moose Lake, Minnesota, in 1931 and lived in Kettle River, Minnesota, until age ten. Home was a small chicken farm in a clearing just east of town. Rollie and his brother, John, spent much time exploring the nearby woods of mostly aspen and birch. The 1918 forest fire had burned most of the white pine. They moved to Columbia Heights, Minnesota, during World War II where his father worked as a machinist.

In 1945 they moved to a home on South Center Lake in Center City, Minnesota. Rollie attended the University of Minnesota graduating with a degree in Geography in 1954. He served two years as an artillery officer in Fort Bliss, Texas, and Kaiserslautern, Germany. Instead of returning to the US, he took his discharge in Germany and traveled around Europe for 14 months. There he met Fred Baas who had the distributorship for Framus Guitars for the U.S.

Rollie moved to Philadelphia and helped Fred start the Philadelphia Music Co. When his mother died in 1960 he moved back to Minnesota and took over a Midwest area for music sales. In 1983 Rollie turned his territory over to his employee and became Ski School Director at Trollhaugen Ski Area so that he would be home more with Martha, and his children, Britta and Peter. Rollie had been an avid skier all his life and has been a member of Professional Ski Instructors of America for over 50 years. Across the years he frequently taught skiing on weekends and did some pro ski racing.

He is one of only a few ski instructors to hold the highest level of PSIA certification in alpine, Nordic track and telemark instructing.

Rollie also served as a PSIA examiner for Nordic track and telemark instructors. Rollie continues to enjoy traveling and exploring the out of doors skiing, biking, canoeing, and camping. He currently lives in Salt Lake City with his wife, Martha, and near his children and grandchildren: Jack, Anika, Arthur, and Isaac.

This is his first book.

Made in the USA
Columbia, SC
26 October 2018